Believe, Ask, Act

For my mom, Alice, my first spiritual teacher,
who taught me to think beyond this world.
And my father, Robert, who taught me to be strong
and have my own voice.
And for their spouses, Bob and Christine,
who have accepted me into their hearts.

For my beautiful children, Emily and Ryan,
who bring me joy every day
and whose enthusiasm for life
inspires me to do my best.

For my husband, Chris.
My love for you transcends lifetimes.
Still. More. Always.

For God and Spirit, for showing me the signs
and asking me to listen.
I am forever grateful for your guidance.

CONTENTS

INTRODUCTION:
PUT DOWN THE VISION BOARD

Perhaps like you, I wear a lot of hats. I'm a mom, wife, friend, dog lover, and fan of all things chocolate and doughy. I'm also a psychic medium, intuitive counselor, and spiritual teacher. As you might guess, the primary reason people seek me out isn't for my pet or nutrition advice. It's for real-world guidance that I channel from divine souls on the Other Side, including angels, spirit guides, loved ones, and other evolved beings whose job is to support you in all that you do. I refer to these groups of celestial helpers as our Universal Teams, and they know quite a lot about what it takes to live your best life—whether that means healing a broken heart, finding a job that aligns with your passions, or overcoming a past that holds you back. They're intent on helping humanity live in a way that feels good and true to our souls.

Now what if I said that you, too, can connect to your Team's wisdom and guidance, and that all it requires is to engage three powerful steps that will raise your intuition, connect you to God's energy, and set change in motion when you feel stuck or blocked? I refer to this process as Believe, Ask, and Act, and this book will show you how to use it. My own Team says there are more effective ways than others to establish your beliefs, partner with knowing souls, and reach your goals. These differences determine whether you face obstacles at every turn or follow a smoother road to joy, growth, and learning.

By picking up this book, you've signaled to the universe that you're ready to trust, listen, and work to realize your greatest potential. Please know that I'm not out to convert you to my belief system or insist that I know the "right" way to feel happy or spiritually fulfilled—I have no agenda here. *Believe, Ask, Act* is about *you* and your journey. I can only do what my own spirit guides have asked of me, which is to share what I've been shown will help you live a meaningful life. It's my greatest hope, and God's, that you understand and value who you are, why you're here, and how your choices impact His universe.

The principles behind *Believe, Ask, Act* have helped thousands of my clients connect to the Other Side; break free from obstacles in their spiritual, emotional, and professional lives; and become more empowered and fulfilled by their everyday choices. Call me psychic, but I have a feeling you're next.

DOING IS BELIEVING

Nearly all my new clients come to me with the same complaint, which goes something like this: "I meditate, go to conferences, think positively, post intentions all over my house—and yet I'm not landing the project/spouse/happiness/closure I need. Why isn't the universe cooperating? Are my angels on hiatus? *What is going on?*" This is when their Universal Teams swoop in, sometimes shaking their heads in disbelief, to talk about how working on certain spiritual priorities will release blocks that get in the way of forward motion. I've found that if you listen to this guidance, you become unstuck and life starts to flow again; if you ignore or address only parts of it, the cycle becomes fixed and this energy feeds other problems—think of it like a traffic jam or pileup on the highway. What was once a single block keeps you from happiness in other areas of your life.

Many self-help experts insist that changing your mind-set or expanding your beliefs will be enough to steer you through trials, but I'm here to tell you that cheerful thoughts and a fine inner voice will not do the heavy lifting on their own. This is a common misperception among my clients who become blocked. They spend a lot of time seeking and studying but have little idea of how to get to their next step with deliberate action guided by their angels and spirit guides. Thus, their efforts fall short time and again and leave them feeling hopeless.

When I channel Universal Teams, they often emphasize that life marches on with or without you. It's up to you to make choices that cause you to take action and risks, up to you to move toward your calling and learn lessons that can inform your path. Positive thinking has its place, but it isn't enough. You must establish and practice a belief in a higher power, ask your divine guidance the right questions, and follow their direction. If you go off course, that's okay. You'll reflect on the situation, learn from it, and try again. Without learning and growth, there's no movement. And movement matters. Clients often think that if a goal is "meant to be," the process of reaching it will feel miraculous at every turn. Sometimes that's true. But missteps can also be part of a learning process that takes advantage of your flaws, since doors fly open when you move through challenges. If you had the ability to make ideal decisions 24/7, you'd be orchestrating God's plan as one of His messengers, not learning from them as a human in this world.

In fact, I've been shown that the difference between those who achieve joy and progress toward their goals and those who don't isn't that they meditate more, love more, or write themselves more uncashed checks than the next person. And it's not about leaning harder on the Law of Attraction, because the universe's power is limited if you only change your mind. You must use Believe, Ask, and Act to pursue the fulfillment, meaning, and wholeness you crave.

HOW TO USE THIS BOOK

In *Believe, Ask, Act*, I'll help you do the work that will advance you along your soul's best path. This means taking a break from the vision boards, sharpening your intuition, trusting God's and your Team's guidance, and putting one earthly foot in front of the other to encourage positive change and motion.

Believe, Ask, Act is divided into three sections to help you utilize the steps and understand the context in which they exist. Throughout, I will also share inspiring true stories from my own journey, counseling sessions, and readings to illustrate how Believe, Ask, and Act create tangible results. In Part I, I'll illustrate why and how Believe, Ask, and Act work by sharing how they've shaped my own life. I'll explain your role in the universe and introduce you to the souls in your Universal Team. I'll also break down the steps so you feel prepared to practice them with confidence. In Part II, I'll explain some of the common spiritual priorities that make or break happiness and help you use the three steps to actually release the blocks that occur when you neglect them. By Part III, you'll have honed your instincts and feel so adept at using this practice that you'll be ready to fold it into your everyday life. The more you implement Believe, Ask, and Act, the more it becomes part of you. It reminds me of learning multiplication tables—through repetitive behavior, you just know four times four is sixteen. Likewise, the more you communicate with your Team and see results, the easier it becomes to recognize and trust their guidance. In doing so, you'll increasingly marry your spiritual and worldly selves.

In my work, I rely on highly evolved souls to guide my words. This book is no different. Everything I advise has been channeled from my Team, especially the exercises, tools, and reflections in Part II. These souls were eager to be heard!

It's time to awaken. Pay attention. Understand your role on this plane and what the universe has to offer. I'm shown that a lot of us need the road to fulfillment and happiness clarified and laid out plainly—and that's okay. The process and universal energy embedded in the Believe, Ask, and Act paradigm are your answer. At its core, *Believe, Ask, Act* is about creating your life as your soul intends and learning lessons along the way. You will discover how to utilize free will, how to become attuned to divine guidance, and how to fulfill your greatest desires. It's a remarkable balancing act and one we will now learn how to master together. Let's begin.

PART I

PREPARING for CHANGE and HAPPINESS

CHAPTER 1

Coming Into My Own

The universe is full of surprises, even for a psychic like me. Sometimes I can't believe my life's story includes raising an awesome family, enduring devastating loss, and communicating with enlightened souls on the Other Side. I've come to embrace the unpredictability, chaos, and beauty of it all, which has led to profound happiness—though, trust me, it wasn't always this way. I had to learn how to utilize divine guidance, listen to my intuition, and grow from my experiences to create the life I love.

Every one of us has what I call a Universal Team of Spirit, including angels, spirit guides, departed loved ones, religious deities, and other evolved souls who help you maneuver through life's ups and downs. And during many difficult years, it was my own Team that helped me move forward. As I did, they carefully revealed an effective approach that has taught me to connect with my highest angels and spirit guides, call upon them, and engage their very best guidance. This is the Believe, Ask, and Act process—three simple and powerful steps that hone your intuition, set change in motion, and clear roadblocks that stand in your way to happiness. No matter what challenges I face, these valuable steps are the reason I wake up every day thinking, *I've got this*. It's the most empowering feeling I know.

In this chapter, I'd like to share my story so that you can see how Spirit has helped shape my world since I was a child and continues to do so through Believe, Ask, and Act. In fact, my Team tells me it's no coincidence that they introduced me to the steps during my darkest times. They wanted to make sure I understood every aspect firsthand so that I could compellingly share it with clients, and now with you.

A SPIRITED CHILDHOOD

I've been gradually feeling, seeing, hearing, and dreaming of Spirit since I was five years old, but I wasn't able to truly understand what I sensed or make practical use of it until later in life. These encounters ran the gamut from obscure to creepy to awe-inspiring. My earliest experiences occurred at my uncle's house, where I simply sensed a presence in the basement that made me want to bolt upstairs—it was jarring to feel that "someone" was with me whom I visibly couldn't see. Sometimes I'd look down his hall and feel like a person should be there, though I'd never witness a figure or shadow with my naked eye; my instincts just told me *a being* was hanging around. In retrospect, I believe this was Spirit's way of gently revealing my gift to me—here, I'd feel a soul's presence, which is called *clairsentience*—so I wouldn't become too overwhelmed or scared by the range of my abilities. Had I, say, heard a disembodied voice or seen a full apparition so young, it might have led me to ignore or fear any kind of divine communication and therefore hesitate to pursue my gift as an adult.

During my grade school years, I began having more obvious encounters with the Other Side. Most of them were comforting and related to family, home, and spiritual references that I could understand. For instance, I often dreamed about enormous, magnificent angels. In one dream, I was with my brother Anthony. We were in a giant field, and when we both looked at the sky, it just . . . opened up for us. Amid the ethereal white clouds, I could see the general shape of huge, brightly lit feet walking above me. I remember Anthony telling me to "stop staring" at them, but I just couldn't! That's when a bluish-white angel the size of a skyscraper emerged. And while I couldn't see the details of its face or clothes, I was captivated by its large wings and the gentle, protective feeling I had in its presence. I now know this was Archangel Michael, because he's since shown me his blue light during meditations. Looking back, I believe he was sent by God to hold my attention so that I'd stay open to my future spiritual path.

Around the age of twelve, I had similarly vivid encounters with my great-grandmother Alessandra's soul after she died. We were very close while she was alive, and I loved hearing her stories about what it was like for her to move with her family from Rome to New York. I remember watching her cook meatballs in a cast-iron pan and picking fresh mint and basil with her in the garden. My great-grandmother actually lived with my uncle for many years, and when she passed away, he left the majority of her room intact. I often snuck into this area to feel her presence around me. I'd touch the white and ruby-red rosary beads that still hung on her bedpost, run my hand over her paisley bedspread, and hold a small porcelain doll that usually sat on her dresser. I could feel her energy surround and envelop me as I did, and I knew her soul was with me as I interacted with the objects she'd once adored.

A few startling encounters with Spirit occurred when I was young, too, which often happens to intuitives, though many don't publicly talk about it. When a psychic medium hasn't learned how to establish boundaries, all kinds of energy, some better or "higher" than others, can reveal themselves to her. This first occurred when I was nine years old, and a thick, opaque shadow with a tall, broad form and pointy ears passed outside our living room window. It scared the *bejesus* out of me—I ran upstairs, crying, and told Mom that a scary creature was creeping around the house. This didn't seem to faze her, as she tried to calm me down. What Mom didn't reveal was that she'd serendipitously arranged to have a psychic over the next day, who cleared the negative energy from our home. Mom never told the psychic what I saw; the woman sensed this on her own, and ten years actually passed before Mom even told me about what made the negative energy disappear.

Believe it or not, the experience with the shadow wasn't half as terrifying as when Spirit revealed the extent to which I could forecast sickness and death. During my great-grandmother Alessandra's final month alive, I could smell her illness and impending passing; it was a thick, stale odor. And in my early teens, when my friend Lori and I were at a wedding together, at one point she looked to me as if she were engulfed by a misty gray cloud or aura. I had to squint to see her face. It was confusing because Lori was such an upbeat and joyful person; what I saw wasn't in sync with her personality. I never said a word about it to anyone, but the next day, I was devastated when my mom told me Lori had died from a sudden illness. I'd seen it coming in a way, and the gravity of this realization weighed on me. Having the foresight to know a person might die—yet no capacity to affect such an outcome—was extremely heavy and hard to process, especially as a child.

My abilities continued to open and expand into my late teens, and thankfully the large majority of them were positive and fun. I dreamed of other time periods in France and Italy that I believe were past lives. And when close family members died, they'd playfully pay me a visit. I remember gathering for Sunday dinners with my living family and seeing deceased loved ones at the table, too! My mom is also intuitive, and she and I began having the same dreams about my departed grandmother and my aunt Rose. We could both describe what their hair looked like, what they were wearing, and what they talked about—to a tee.

It had become increasingly clear that I had a stronger intuition than the average bear, and the more I accepted it, the more Spirit validated it. I'd guess songs on the radio before they played or know how a conversation would go down before it happened. With the exception of sensing illness, which I tried my best to tune out, I was no longer startled or surprised when I could exercise my psychic muscle—in fact, I got a real kick out of it! I considered my abilities to be a pretty cool gift that I was born with, the way some can tinkle a song on the piano by ear. But I still couldn't use it consistently or at will.

BEING MY MOTHER'S DAUGHTER

Most of the women in my mom's family are, or were while they were alive, psychic to varying degrees, so I was taught to embrace my random experiences and abilities as part of who I am. This didn't conflict with these women's faiths, since the Northern Italian matriarchs in my life always embraced a cultural blend of spirituality or mysticism and organized religion. So many Italians do, though most don't realize or acknowledge it. For instance, the Italian horn, or *corno*, is meant to protect against the evil eye; it's been said to represent the Virgin Mary standing on a lunar crescent. But even further back, it's thought to symbolize the Old European moon goddess. Or what about Saint Padre Pio? He was an ordained priest who bore the stigmata but also had healing gifts and the ability to read souls like angels.

Though both spiritual and faithful influences were all around me, I was never raised with a religion. My dad didn't subscribe to one, and after Mom gave birth to me and my brother, she left Catholicism and embarked on her own spiritual quest. Our family celebrated Christian holidays like Christmas and Easter, but Mom referred to God as an energetic higher power that created the universe. As early as grade school, she taught me to believe in spiritual teachers like Jesus and Buddha—or "higher masters," as she called them—spirit guides, angels, and the idea that our souls graduate to different planes of consciousness when we die. During elementary school, I attended spirituality conferences with Mom, and we'd meditate together almost every night. During this, she said I should see colors or images in my "third eye," or "mind's eye," though I never could. I did learn the practice of being still while other kids threw tantrums, and on weekends, Mom and I would wonder what God had in store as many churchgoers were told the best stuff already happened. Mom kept her mind open to new metaphysical theories and inspired me to do the same.

So imagine Mom's complete and utter *thrill* when she went to see a reputable psychic medium named John Edward—young, talented, and still working out of his mother's basement in Long Island. She was referred by a friend at work. I was about eighteen at the time, and during her reading, he told Mom that I, too, was a medium who hadn't learned to hone her skills yet. Though she wasn't too surprised, Mom was so excited to tell me this. John might as well have said I'd become a doctor! This was a fascinating validation for me, as well, because when I'd meet psychics through my mom, a voice inside would say, "You can do that," but it felt silly to admit this aloud.

Since I was on the cusp of adulthood, it was cool to hear a psychic reveal that I had such a wild future ahead of me. And while I'd met gifted intuitives through my mom, I didn't know there was a distinct group of them that could connect with the afterlife the way John does. He knew details about my family's past, present, and future—all from departed loved ones—that were so accurate, it blew Mom away. So for him to say our abilities were similar? This was like hitting the cosmic jackpot for a spiritual mom and her curious daughter. *A medium!* I thought. *That's what I'm called!* And then: *Holy crap. How do I learn to do this?*

I began to search for more information about what lay ahead of me, but I couldn't get a handle on how one is meant to hone *any* intuitive ability, much less spin it into a fulfilling life. I tried using tarot cards, but I couldn't get them to work. I meditated every day, hoping for an epiphany or vision, but I saw only the backs of my eyelids. I attended a few Spiritualist events, but at that age, I couldn't relate to their woo-woo vibe. I read metaphysical books about stating intentions, but they never told me how to act on them, so I put those aside and picked up memoirs by famous mediums like Sylvia Browne and James Van Praagh. These were always fascinating, but they didn't offer the practical answers I craved.

Back in the real world, I was in my twenties, working long hours in the retail industry and going out at night. Clearly, the psychic thing wasn't panning out as I'd hoped, though I still had an uncanny sense for when I was about to get a raise and could give a friend spot-on advice that'd later come to fruition. I also continued to dream of angels and have mind-blowing premonitions. I'll never forget when I was cruising down the highway with a friend and heard a voice inside me say, "Pull over. There's going to be an accident." Just as I did—*bam!*—a small black compact slammed into a massive tractor trailer, right where my car had been seconds earlier.

This was all really helpful and fascinating to me, but again, I wanted to sharpen my intuitive abilities and be able to use them in a consistent way—though Spirit had no plans to hand me my road map anytime soon. In fact, I remember a dream I had where I was sitting on a sofa next to my grandmother's soul as she was quietly knitting, and I asked her about my gift. She responded by placing her index finger over her lips, like the old lady whispering *hush* in *Goodnight Moon.*

GETTING A GRIP ON GOD

By my midtwenties, I put my spiritual search aside, got married, and gave birth to a gorgeous daughter and son. Before she was born, I dreamed about my little girl at six months old and smiled at a tiny beauty mark she still has on the top of her head. After she was born, I dreamed I was pregnant again, but this time, I saw a baby floating in utero and it made me feel queasy. I sensed this child wouldn't flourish, and I was very upset when I lost it. Then I got pregnant a third time, and when I was only a few weeks in, I was drifting in and out of a nap on my sofa, and I could literally hear a toddler's feet pattering around me as he giggled and laughed! My mom was visiting, and when I woke up, she said, "You have a little boy running around. He came right up to my face!" It was still too early to know the child's sex, but sure enough, my vivacious son was born seven months later.

Maybe because my parents divorced when I was thirteen, I had idealistic hopes for what my marriage and family would be like. After my daughter was born, I hurried to quit my job, stayed home with the kids, and became furiously protective of them—I was a proud mama bear, if ever there was one. To be honest, I still am. I loved playing house and adored everything about being a mother and wife, but when I hit my thirties, my happiness began to shift. I faced frustrating health issues, threw myself into more activities than I could manage, and realized that beyond loving and living for my kids, I was trying to busy myself because life felt a bit empty.

I also never stopped grieving my failed pregnancy, and I think that impacted my marriage more than my husband and I admitted at the time. Somewhere between me juggling my responsibilities as head of the PTA and an appointed member of the school board, and my husband trying to balance his work and home life, we disconnected and drifted apart. We stopped communicating, and my self-esteem took a nosedive. I felt like I was disappearing, and I couldn't tell you who I was anymore. It was a confusing time for us both, and I found many hours of solace in pints of vanilla moose tracks.

Yet no matter how blue I felt, I knew deep inside that my muted and mixed-up day-to-day existence was *not* my fate—I knew I wasn't living true to myself. And while I sensed there was more for me, I didn't know how to find or achieve it. For example, I tried the daytime talk show approach of embarking on a regimen to boost my self-esteem that included running, holistic health, and spending quality time with girlfriends. But in my heart, I knew acupuncture and appletinis could only do so much, and my problems were too messy to untangle on my own. It was a dizzying reality for me, when all I wanted was to feel safe, grounded, and truly content. I thought about how my picket-fence fantasies had failed me, my self-improvement efforts fell short, and the spiritual compasses I'd tried to use and understand let me down.

A still, small voice inside said it was time to turn to God in a new way—at least for me.

I began to pray. A *lot*. Since I wasn't raised with religion, I didn't know exactly what to say or how to address Him—I just did what came naturally. On my knees every night, I asked God for help in a way that felt comfortable. I had what felt like a conversation that placed a request and expressed gratitude in anticipation of an answer. My prayers changed depending on the day, but they mostly circled the words *Thank you for telling me what I need to do. Thank you for showing me my next steps and protecting my kids during whatever you have in mind.* I'd sense a response that would guide me to baby steps that felt like progress. For example, one night after asking to be shown a support system during this hard time, it dawned on me that

I might enjoy being part of a church. My daughter had been enrolled in Catholic school for four years at this point, yet I never paused to understand what she was learning. I realized we might both benefit from taking our God journey together. So I visited three parishes in town until I found the best fit for me. I took classes with the priest, who taught me about God's ways and was there for me when I needed advice. I nourished my belief system and found a lot of peace in the church's structure and community. At the Easter Vigil that first year, I received communion and confirmation (my daughter was still too young for either). The forward motion felt encouraging.

As all this unfolded, I felt divine guidance at work; each step came with a soft prod to keep going and a sense that everything was going to be okay—maybe not immediately ideal, but doable. I know now that having sudden good ideas, feeling drawn to uncanny choices, and receiving calm validations that you're on the right track are all ways that Spirit leads you through intuition. For me, I think that being spiritually open from childhood and finding a church that insisted I could have a relationship with a loving God helped me invest in a belief system that I could get behind. And then actively trusting God encouraged me to examine and pursue the feelings, conversations, and opportunities that arose, because I felt that between His guidance and my choices, I'd land where I needed to be.

During this time, it also became increasingly clear that I had to address my marriage. I'd been paying closer attention to my feelings, hearing arguments in a more realistic light, and feeling my husband's distance in a new way. When he and I met, I was a pleaser and fixer, and I loved him enough to try to figure out how to make our marriage work. But the more I grew, the more I craved a natural emotional connection we didn't have. I wasn't happy, and it wasn't fair to either of us to go on like this.

I remember telling my priest how upset I was to consider divorce, and I couldn't believe how he responded. "God wants you to be happy," he said. "He's not sitting in Heaven, judging whether you're playing by the rules every day. Do what you need to do to feel good." That was so freeing, I can't tell you. I felt that my kids deserved a lighthearted and goofy mom, not a depressed one. I went back to work, and my husband and I separated. We continued to parent as a team but under different roofs. I'm not going to lie—it was hard at first. I had more bad days than good, trying not to question our choice or look over my shoulder. I felt lonely and wondered how our relationship would affect the kids long term.

Then a few months after my husband left, he called to say that his father, James, had fallen from a ladder and onto his concrete driveway. I typically don't panic in a crisis—I'm calm under pressure and usually the one who figures things out. But when I heard about the accident, I frantically called my friend Corinne to insist she come stay with the kids. I *knew* something was very wrong and that I needed to be with my in-laws. The medics airlifted James to a nearby hospital, and we learned that the fall caused a life-threatening brain injury.

James was in a coma for six weeks, and then he passed away. His death was a tragic, devastating blow for our entire family, as he was such a strong father figure to all of us. James was always front and center at the kids' games and recitals, joined us on vacation every year, and visited on a daily basis. I loved him so much, and he and my mother-in-law, with whom I'm still close, were inseparable. I already felt tremendous guilt over my failed marriage, and telling the kids that their grandfather died was the last thing I wanted to do. They'd cried enough, and now this. I was also a mess. Between James's unexpected death and the separation, it felt like the world was ending. But the collective blow put so much in perspective that, while my husband and I did finalize the divorce, we haven't really fought since.

My own journey through the Believe, Ask, and Act process had begun to take shape, though I didn't connect my experiences with those words at the time. But through the confusion, grief, and emotional displacement, I had faith, asked for guidance, and acted on the direction I felt—even when I had to work through heartache and frustration to get to my goals. I leaned on divine guidance while claiming responsibility for how I lived. I came to terms with my divorce, which also meant overcoming a tremendous amount of fear and enduring painful gossip from some friends and family members. I stepped outside my comfort zone and trusted that even terrifying risks can lead to progress. And I just continued moving forward, with a growing faith in the universe. I also found that the more I prayed, the harder my challenges became—not because God was testing me, but because I was being honest about what I needed to do and could see clearly that the path wouldn't be easy. I expressed gratitude anyway and removed all time frames from what I was about to learn or encounter next.

Although it wasn't an easy move, I could feel that I was in the driver's seat of my life, acting on the directions that God and His emissaries sent me.

About a month after my father-in-law passed, I felt led to make two additional, pivotal moves. I began to spend more time with an old friend named Chris and revisit my interests in honing my instincts and psychic abilities. I knew these choices were guided, because they felt good in a way that reminded me of how I felt when I made other wise decisions that had worked out for the best. I also felt a mix of positive anticipation and butterflies, which I now know is how Spirit energy feels when it channels through me.

THERE ARE NO COINCIDENCES

I met a spiritual teacher from Long Island named Pat Longo through a mixed-up referral, and here's where my story came together for me. I was actually scheduled to see another now-famous celebrity medium, but she had to cancel at the last minute, and so my friend who'd referred me to her suggested I see Pat instead. She thought Pat was this woman's psychic, so I was game—a famous psychic's psychic? I'm in! But when I called Pat, she explained she was a spiritual teacher and healer, not a psychic, and the medium was once her student. She asked if I wanted to cancel, but I felt that this coincidence, coupled with my stalled efforts to understand my abilities, was about to make sense.

"Nope, I'm supposed to come see you," I said. "I know it."

During our visit, I shared my entire history with Pat, including my premonitions and dreams. She asked if I could "hear Spirit," and I had no idea what she meant. Once in a while I'd hear an audible voice when I was the only person in the room, but I didn't chat up ghosts all day. "Spirit comes in your own voice," she clarified, further explaining that souls mostly use our instincts and inner voice to communicate with us. That's when, out of nowhere, I heard my own inner voice say *Mention the A-name*—and when I repeated it to Pat, she said her deceased mom's name is Alice. Get out of town!

Pat took this psychic validation as a cue to perform a healing on me. She asked me to close my eyes and she placed her hands over my body. She channeled energy from her angels and spirit guides to improve my physical, mental/emotional, and spiritual health. This process can also open intuitive doorways, so to speak, which is what happened next.

"Tell me if you see, hear, or feel anything," Pat said.

I told her I felt a peacefulness wash over me. My eyes were shut, but I saw purple, blue, and green waves swirling around like a lava lamp in my third eye (Mom would be proud!). Pat said the colors corresponded to the awakening of my chakras: Purple represents spiritual awareness, my third eye expanding, and the ability to see clairvoyantly. Blue symbolizes my ability to communicate and express myself. And green stands for my capacity to offer compassion, love, and healing to others. For Pat, the colors helped validate which of my intuitive abilities were about to become the most active in my life.

After doing her thing, Pat moved across the room so I could sit alone with my eyes still closed. *This is fun but kind of nuts*, I thought—and remembering this now, I can almost hear my angels and spirit guides laugh, *You ain't seen nothin' yet!* Things got crazier real fast. I was facing a glass door, and even with my eyes shut, I could see golden sunlight streaming through. Then all of a sudden, I saw a figure emerge from the wall to my right and block out the light from the doorway. Standing in front of me was a full apparition of my father-in-law, James. He looked so young and vibrant! He wore a blue-and-white-striped shirt and denim jeans, and he had long hair and an eighties mustache like when he was young. I started to cry.

"It's time to use your gift," James said to me. "You're ready now. I'll be back." He smiled and walked out of the room. In life and in death, he's a no-nonsense guy.

"What the hell was that?" I asked Pat, after telling her what happened.

"You're a medium," she said, calm but giddy. "Are you ready for the ride of your life?"

For the next year, I traveled almost two hours to Pat's group classes to feverishly learn everything I could about how to finally grow, control, and use my abilities. I did my homework and followed her instructions to the letter. Most importantly, I learned to trust what I was sensing and the information I was delivering—no matter how crazy it felt to do this for a stranger, without any context whatsoever. Can you imagine saying to someone you've never met, "Your dad is standing next to you, incredibly well dressed, and I can smell his musky cologne. He wants to thank you for the pocket watch you placed in his coffin"—and then having that same person break down in tears and say, "Oh, my gosh, you're describing my dad perfectly!"? It made me feel good to help people in this way, and at the same time, it felt like a validating relief to finally do what I always felt and was told I was capable of doing.

The next chapter of my life was unfolding. For the first time in years, I felt at home in my body, mind, and soul—guided, all along, by God and Spirit. I noticed, too, that as I took leaps of faith in this area, my personal life came together. My kids felt more settled and their sadness was lifting; my ex had moved on; and my friend Chris turned out to be the great love of my life. It felt so soothing to know that deep, genuine, and absolute love not only existed but existed for me. I'd met my soul's true partner. The kids embraced Chris wholeheartedly, and two years later, we married. Our family was complete.

BEING AN A+ STUDENT

In Pat's class, I learned about the Other Side (or Heaven, as I also like to call it), how to hone my instincts with understanding and exactitude, and how to live a more spiritually balanced life. One of the first things she taught us is that there's a thin, invisible veil that exists between our world and the Other Side. Souls are made of energy, which has different frequencies depending on what state it's in—a soul in Heaven operates on a higher frequency, while human energy is lower. When I channel, my consciousness and Spirit's consciousness meet in the middle, which is why psychics like me are called mediums. Pat also pointed out that one's faith and spirituality should complement each other, as they both reinforce a belief in a higher power and underscore the importance of practicing forgiveness, gratitude, trust, and refraining from all judgment. She insisted that I utilize, share, and embrace my abilities without guilt, shame, ego, and fear and that I use them to lovingly serve others because they are a gift from God.

In class, I also learned to communicate with Spirit in a safe and protected way that allowed me to receive and translate messages from the Other Side. In order to do this work, Pat said I had to establish boundaries with Spirit during meditation so that I could always feel comfortable with the sensations they impressed upon me. The first thing I specified was that I no longer wanted to experience major illness, death, or negativity— it freaked me out when I was young, and I asked Spirit to take that away. It worked!

A very constructive part of Pat's instruction involved reading other students for practice. I'd been to only three sessions when, one morning, I heard a voice in the shower. It was my own voice, but it *felt* like it was coming from a man. Unlike in the past, the voice did not come from my head or my gut; it spoke *into* my inner ear. Tuning in to this sound reminded me of trying to tune in on a radio station—I could hear bits and pieces of a message, and when I remembered from class how to access the actual voice, it came in loud and clear.

"Uh, hello?" the voice said.

"Hello?" I answered aloud, rushing to shut off the water, jump out of the shower, and cover myself with a towel. I grabbed a pen and pad in the bedroom and began taking notes on what the soul wanted to relay. It turned out to be a message for a classmate from his deceased father. When

I delivered it that night, my friend assured me that every word resonated. I couldn't believe how far I'd come! In no time at all, I was able to hear Spirit in my head and ear (known as clairaudience), see them with my naked eye and mind's eye, or third eye (clairvoyance), and feel them around or touch me (clairsentience). Though I tap three heightened senses when I channel, every intuitive is different in how they sense Spirit.

Though I've always been the friend you turn to for advice and guidance, I always thought this was because I'm a loudmouthed Italian with strong opinions. Now, I realize this is as much my personality as it is part of my soul's best path! The fact that I'm often right may have little to do with me, because I think I've been inadvertently channeling guided opinions longer than I realize! Between Spirit's direction and my gift of gab, we're quite a team. I thank God every day for leading me to Pat's capable hands.

Though I'd brought my consciousness to a whole new level, a lot of what I now knew to be true simply reinforced what I'd been taught about the universe at a very young age. Remember, I had always sensed Spirit to some degree, so I wasn't so much astonished that Heaven was for real as I was excited to connect with the souls that called it home. What amazed me most at the time, and still does, is that the messages I deliver are consistently correct, purposeful, and detailed. Am I in complete awe when Spirit predicts a pregnancy, takes a client's hand during a reading, and creates signs and scenarios that guide us all on our soul's best path? Absolutely. But I try not to get caught up in the wow factor associated with what I do. It's delicate work to channel for grief-stricken clients and those in need of life's direction. It's also enormously humbling and rewarding to know it's my soul's purpose to work in conjunction with the universe this way.

SHOW ME THE SPIRIT!

After I finished class, I began to see clients in my home office to channel messages from departed loved ones, and once I felt comfortable with this, Spirit quickly expanded my abilities even more. During my clients' readings,

I began communicating with the souls that guide them—their Universal Teams—and many sessions became counseling oriented. Sometimes Spirit would start dispensing guidance halfway through a mediumship reading with loved ones; other times, clients would specifically schedule an intuitive counseling session to address, say, an impending business deal or relationship issue. I'm a firm believer that Spirit always gives you the messages you need, since it's their job to love, protect, and guide you in life. This perhaps explains a third group of people who'd book a mediumship session and quickly learn that a loved one was actually part of their Team and wanted to talk about a client's personal roadblocks!

No matter how much my clients appreciate the information that helps them create change and happiness, they can't help but wonder what I *see*. I don't blame them—it's a fascinating reveal for me, too! So here's the deal. It takes a lot of energy to appear as a 3-D apparition, so the way James came to me, for instance, doesn't happen a lot. I mostly see Spirit with my eyes open but in front of me with my third eye; in both scenarios, I tend to see messages play out like a movie or slide show. I can also sustain an energetic image with my third eye much longer than if I see it with the naked eye, which is helpful.

If I do see images with my naked eye, I'm usually floored. Once, I read a client who'd lost her dad. In the middle of my driveway, clear as day, I saw a solid flagpole waving an American flag—seconds later, it was gone! This made me think of the Fourth of July, and that was the soul's birthday, which is why Spirit showed me the image. And when there's a lot of energy in the room, it turns cloudy or misty to my naked eye. I might also see flashes of white light, as Spirit prepares for me to channel them.

When souls on your Team are in Spirit form, their energy is pure light; however, they present themselves to me in a way that jives with how you remember them if they're loved ones, or if they're higher beings, your belief system and/or a former lifetime of theirs. A grandfather, for example, might appear as white light but wear recognizable glasses and a hat so that you can verify his identity. Or if you're Catholic, I might see angels with wings—particularly with archangels—because that's a familiar biblical image. Yet in meditation, archangels have dropped their "skin" to me and appeared as colored light. If I'm channeling for a Hindu, I'm not going to see Jesus but maybe Ganesh. Egyptians, Grecians, Native Americans, Tibetan monks, and religious figures can also guide you, as can the souls of beings who lived on other planets. This last group can guide you from the Other Side just like earthly guides who once lived here and do their work from Heaven. Don't freak out: Planetary guides have souls of light, created by God, just like you and me. They have wonderful intentions and are all about positivity.

As I listen carefully to Universal Teams, I may take on their traits, mannerisms, gestures, and tone as I translate what they say. I mostly hear a quick and quiet word, feeling, or sentence that arrives in my thoughts and voice. I know these don't come from me because they aren't loud and don't follow a train of thought the way ideas that come from the mind do. Spirit's words are usually disconnected from what comes before and after them. Sometimes I can also hear words or have conversations at the same time that I'm talking to a client; please don't ask how I do this, because I have no clue. Spirit may talk fast or slow, depending on what their energetic vibration is. If I don't get what they're saying, I ask Spirit to work harder—I like to channel specifics I couldn't know any other way. What's more, I've developed a "vocabulary" with spiritual beings to make things easy. Beyond words, they use symbols, sounds, feelings, and smells that help me communicate what they want me to say. For instance, when Spirit jingles the sound of keys in my ear, this cues me to mention that the client may be selling their home, or if a soul shows me a train, that the person I'm reading will be taking a trip.

Today, one of the things I love about communicating with Universal Teams is that I meet incredible energies that emanate goodness, love, and reassurance. The information they share is always positive and for the well-being of my client and humanity at large. These Teams have never led me or my clients astray. Through this work, I've broadened my beliefs to include a larger understanding of the universe, which I'll explain in the next chapter—and I like that it doesn't negate my belief system but builds on it. A lot of what Spirit shows me is similar to what I was taught as a child and later learned in church. I've never doubted Spirit's intentions or the guidance I channel from the Teams that look out for our best interests.

Though I had the ability to communicate with Spirit my whole life, my Team assures me that I was guided to hone my gift at the "right time." As a psychic medium and intuitive counselor, I needed to develop my empathy and cultivate life experiences that I could draw on to deliver messages. I had to know what it was to feel fear, loss, loneliness, and insecurity so that I could relate to clients whose lives are at a frustrating or heartbreaking halt. I had to demonstrate that I could give and receive love again through my new marriage. I had to let go of doubt and fear, discover my inner strength, and take meaningful risks. I had to know what it felt like to get knocked down, brush myself off, and keep going with an awareness of and appreciation for God and His messengers in Spirit.

BRINGING BELIEVE, ASK, AND ACT TO YOU

In order to bring Believe, Ask, and Act to you, my Universal Team assures me that I had to walk the walk of the three steps. This doesn't mean they caused my divorce, losses, and other trying experiences so that I could deliver their message—that would be awful! They simply waited until I encountered big challenges to unveil a process that led to learning and growth. If I'd married another man or not lost a father figure, a different series of obstacles would surely have arisen—we all face these—to prompt me to crystallize my beliefs, communicate with my Team, and learn how to move forward (in Chapter 3, I'll talk further about what Spirit can and can't control in the course of your life). No matter when or how the dark night of my soul came about, Spirit knew that I had to go through this period to grasp and communicate Believe, Ask, and Act. Remember, the process was not easier for me because I'm a medium—I had to make the most of stops and starts, just like you. But I emerged with a stronger intuition and awareness of how to navigate life's complexities, and if you use Believe, Ask, and Act, I'm shown you'll experience the same. Okay, so maybe you won't come out of this a psychic, but you *will* hear from your Team and feel fortified to make the most of your time on this marvelous earth.

I continue to use Believe, Ask, and Act to maintain a connection to my Team and travel my soul's best path, and I've shown thousands of clients how to do the same. The three steps won't make you coast through life, but they will help you navigate its twists and turns in every area—from relationships to finances to career. Change will feel exciting and come naturally. Joy becomes a reality. Are you ready?

CHAPTER 2

Your Role in God's Universe

First things first, it's essential that you understand your role in the universe and how it relates to Believe, Ask, and Act. Your happiness is vital to your life, soul, and the experiences of those around you as well as the universe's function. When you feel and spread happiness in big and small ways—from launching a passion project to exchanging smiles with a stranger on the street—your positivity creates a dynamic vibration that emanates from your soul, and this energy helps the earthly plane operate and powers the universe. Because the three steps help guide you through challenges and roadblocks, they will in turn help you boost your happiness, create more positivity, and have far-reaching effects on humanity.

In this chapter, I'm going to pull back the curtain to show you how valuable you are in the greater context of God's universe. I'll share what Spirit has told me about the importance of following your soul's best path, learning lessons, growing your consciousness, and spreading positivity. When you use Believe, Ask, and Act to overcome challenges and uphold spiritual priorities, you live in a way that makes you feel good but also keeps the universe in motion. Your happiness, then, is both a divine gift and responsibility.

YOU'RE HERE TO LIVE YOUR SOUL'S BEST PATH

Every living thing has a soul. Our souls live in our bodies while we're on earth as humans and without them on the Other Side after we die. All souls are made of energy—a pure, beautiful light that's created from God's energy and radiates from within us. Because energy cannot be created or destroyed, I believe that my brain is wired in such a way that I can tap into these soulful energies at any time.

Your soul empowers you to take action, achieve goals, and appreciate your time on this plane when you listen to and act on your instincts. Your instincts live in your soul and operate as a life compass that becomes more exact as you use it. It's your Team's job to communicate through this compass to help align you with your soul's best path. Listening to your instincts, and thus your Team, cuts a clear path to happiness.

Your soul's path is generally informed by impressions from past lives and your current one—think of it like a fingerprint that's uniquely yours but also constantly evolving with each journey on earth. Just as a fingerprint is made up of tiny ridges, whorls, and loops, your soul has imprints formed from good and bad experiences, memories, personality traits, lessons, and other details that influence your identity in each lifetime. For instance, if you liked being an artist or healer in a past life, you might carry those gifts into this one and perhaps choose to use them as a gallery owner or doctor. You're free, of course, to pursue choices that throw you off your soul's path, but your imprint is meant to help you live in a way that feels good and true. This is what some psychics define as a purpose or calling, and I'm shown that it's never just one thing. Being a medium, mom, and friend, for instance, are all part of the genuine and ever-evolving me. God wants you to use every facet of who you are to live your most satisfying life—one that makes you happy, grows your soul, and emanates the positivity that feeds the universe's very existence.

My client Eleanor first came to me for a reading when she lost her brother. After his soul reassured her he was content and at peace on the Other Side, he told me Eleanor had a good life—a strong marriage, loving children, impressive home—but that she wasn't living her passion, and that ate at her. I knew where this was going, and I could tell this soul was part of Eleanor's Team. He told me she constantly asked herself, "What am I good at? What should I be doing?" and then gave me the words "interior design." I asked Eleanor if she'd ever thought about decorating. "I've always had it in the back of my mind . . . ," she mused. Her brother's message articulated what he saw on her soul's imprint.

For three more years, Eleanor saw me for readings—not counseling—yet her brother would not let her forget about that decorating bug! Then one day, Eleanor's Facebook update appeared in my feed and said she'd launched an interior design business. I couldn't wait to congratulate her for listening to her brother and, more importantly, her soul. All the nudging and self-questioning Eleanor felt was from her Team reminding her that she'd feel so happy if she used the creativity she brought into this world. When Eleanor listened to what she felt inside, prompted by her instincts and Team's urging, she felt complete.

A lot of psychics feel that every detail of your soul's path is predetermined, but I'm shown that between birth and death, there are no fixed markers that you will absolutely hit on your way to an inevitable destination. You script your life story time and again. Who will determine it? You or the elements around you? Even detours have meaning when you thoughtfully navigate them. Your choices help define your best path, allowing it to reroute and adapt according to a mix of free will and guidance. This means you have the freedom to do what feels right plus the responsibility to own those choices. All the while, your Team lends a hand if you ask, because they want you to thrive and it's their job to guide you. They're a motivated and productive support system tasked to help you excel. Their hope is that you'll ultimately make sound choices that create the happiness that affects you and the world around you.

YOU'RE HERE TO LEARN LESSONS

One goal of all souls is to learn lessons that evolve their consciousness, and Spirit has shown me there are five main concepts under which all lessons fall. They are: getting over fear, releasing doubt, giving and receiving love, expressing gratitude, and trusting in God and the universe. For that reason, you'll notice that these concepts course throughout *Believe, Ask, Act* and, in some cases, are so important that Spirit led me to devote an entire chapter to a single one of these ideas. How these lesson concepts play out in a lifetime is different for everyone. For instance, overcoming fear is one of the hardest and most significant lessons you can learn. But a mom might overcome fear by not helicopter-parenting her son in this life based on the subconscious fact that she lost a child in a past one, while a teenager might conquer fear for the first time by standing up to a bossy friend. Don't over-think the Big Five, but do be mindful of them as they surface in your life. It feels good to excel in these areas, and your efforts are revered when you cross over.

Many spiritual folks feel that predetermined situations are meant to teach you lessons, but I'm shown that your Team distributes lessons based on your life's circumstances. You learn from navigating a challenge not from the incident itself. Your spirit guides and angels determine how life lessons unfold within certain age windows, but nothing's a given. Early experiences inform future choices and lessons, and Spirit makes adjust-ments according to your actions and the events that happen *to* you. The only exception to this are the dates of your birth and death, but the details in between are malleable. Because of free will, your timeline evolves as you mature, learn, and change or don't, though Spirit always tries to get you back on track and to work in conjunction with your choices so you can learn as much as possible.

I want to be clear that I do *not* believe that your soul, while still in Heaven, chooses any kind of negative circumstance in order to learn. I'm shown that traumas, natural disasters, and bad turns are part of this plane and include Third World poverty, abuse, addiction, illness, and the like. It breaks my heart when clients ask if their child's leukemia or spouse's car accident was predestined to teach a lesson or inspire them to pay it forward by, say, launching a nonprofit. As with all tragedies, this is not the case. What Spirit does say is that by starting a nonprofit, you turn a challenging situation into an inspiring one, which might teach you generosity, love, and how to overcome fear. That's where the lessons come in.

God doesn't "test" you, either. Your Team may create opportunities that give you the chance to make choices that help you grow or tee up a lesson based on what's already going on in your life, but it's not your Team's job to determine how your life ultimately works out. Guided moments might even feel upsetting at the time (such as a series of frustrating incidents at work) but work out for the best when you ask Spirit for help (you find a better job). No matter what, you must use your free will to make wise and informed choices by following the instinctual feelings, signs, and guidance that your Team offers.

My client Jo's life has been full of ups and downs, but she always emerges from pitfalls with gusto and grows from them each time. Jo grew up poor, married young, and found herself in an abusive marriage. She divorced her husband and raised their child alone, which was challenging for her, but years later, she met another man and married him. He loved her unconditionally and offered her financial security to boot. Just when Jo thought she could exhale, this man lost all his money in a series of poor business deals. So to help support their family, Jo decided to launch her own cosmetic supply company—and don't you know, its current estimated worth is in the millions! Life was good for a while, but when her son fell in with a bad crowd, Jo began taking antianxiety meds that caused scary side effects. As soon as she realized the connection, Jo swore off all toxins, began a new exercise routine, and got her life back on the upswing.

It'd be easy for Jo to gripe that God dealt her a capricious hand, that a black cloud follows her around, or that her soul signed up for drama, but that's not what I'm shown. Jo's choices led her to situations that allowed her to learn love, strength, gratitude, and how to overcome fear through her own actionable effort. After her last reading, Jo told me that she'd begun seeing a cognitive behavioral therapist to understand how her emotions, thoughts, and behaviors affect each other so that she can do even more to *stay* on a positive track. I was thrilled for her! As you'll read in Chapter 4, Spirit encourages us to use worldly resources like therapy to be happy, since they can guide us through other people's input and advice.

It's mostly when you choose to *stop* learning that you hit major roadblocks and get stuck in a spiritual revolving door. These are my clients who walk through life with their heads in the sand, giving off negative energy and repeating patterns. You may know people like this and describe them with phrases like "ignores the obvious" and "beats a dead horse." You may even be one of them! Clients who don't learn will ignore their instincts or let fear and doubt rule their lives, which is no way to live at all.

Life is what *you* make of it, and your choices impact the way energy flows around you now and in the future. Remember, your soul's path is the sum of your deeds over an abundance of years and many incarnations; in all these lives, you had freedom of choice. Your current life represents all your past experiences, positive and unpleasant, so you're always the product of your former free-will choices. Your Team supports you, but they won't open every door or hand you a pot of gold. They're with you to aid in self-reflection and stir your core self. You and only you can allow yourself to head in the best direction.

In fact, when I read or "predict" a person's future, what I actually see are the goals you are setting for yourself and have been guided toward based on how your choices compare to your imprint. It's not an ephemeral prediction, pulled out of thin air. Spirit actually shows me if you're following or ignoring their direction. This is to say, I see your soul's *potential* in this life, but whether your hopes and interests come to fruition is largely up to you. If I read a mom and explain what's possible for her child, it usually suits the child's personality or reflects a choice the child made that has set wheels in motion. But that child can also make choices that throw him off his path. This reminds me of myself. John Edward told my mom that I was a medium when I was a kid—he saw the potential—but it wasn't until my late thirties that I began doing what he said I "could" do. It happened when I established a belief system, followed guidance and honed my instincts, and acted on what I was told. It happened when I used Believe, Ask, and Act.

YOU'RE HERE TO LIVE POSITIVELY

I'm sure you've heard the saying "Happiness makes the world go 'round"—and when happiness is fueled by positivity, this couldn't be truer. That's because your positivity creates an enormous ripple effect that has tangible benefits for the universe. Spirit says a positive feeling turns into a positive thought, which becomes a positive intention and then a positive action—and all of this good stuff puts positive energy into the universe. The end result is a literal, energetic vibration or pulse that helps the world and every life-form in it to function, including yours, other people's, nature's, and the energy on the Other Side. "There's a common cause that runs through every plane and level of consciousness," my guides told me, "and that is to keep feeding the universe love and light, and running with a positive tone."

To emanate positivity, Spirit says to focus on thinking, feeling, and demonstrating pleasing emotions like joy, calm, gratitude, amusement, generosity, kindness, optimism, and a healthy perspective because all of these create a happy effect within and around you. Now the Law of Attraction says that if you concentrate on positive thoughts and actions, you will attract positive results (ditto for negative thoughts and actions). While I'm shown that's somewhat true in an energetic sense, as with the Buddhist who puts positive intentions into the world through meditation, it's not the whole story. Real-world positive actions are just as essential; much of why the Law of Attraction works is because when you turn kind and upbeat actions on others, it makes them feel good and encourages them to reciprocate. Positive efforts and attitudes are spiritually contagious—think of how a happy person puts others at ease when he walks into a room and encourages those around him to follow suit. The energy behind his actions spreads like chicken pox, except you itch to feel as good as he does, and so you follow his example! One of Spirit's favorite ways for us to act positively is to pay it forward. It can be as small a gesture as when my client Faith quietly picked up the tab for a serviceman's family at a diner where she was eating, to thank him for serving our country.

What I'm not advocating is for you to adopt a Goody Two-Shoes attitude or push down sad or angry feelings during a painful time; Spirit's the first to say this is unrealistic and disingenuous. When all feels lost, you don't even have to look on the bright side if it's too difficult. Better to express gratitude for one thing in your life—a pet's love, a reliable babysitter, a good Zumba workout—because that single, positive acknowledgment will boost and brighten your soul's energy. Or try to muster a prayer or compliment, since its positive ripple effects touch others.

I have five go-to practices that always lift my soul in a positive way, and I encourage you to try them, too. The first is to take five minutes every morning to thank God and your Team for the blessings in your life—family, friends, or just a good cup of coffee. I also like to create and/or go to a happy place in real life or in my mind. You can designate a room in your home that makes you smile, head to a calm setting like a beach or water-fall, or visualize a peaceful spot to "visit" during meditation or a daydream. The third is to use meditation, prayer, and cathartic exercises like reading and writing—no matter where you do them—to make you feel uplifted. A fourth option for when you're on the go or short on time is to imagine a golden cord connecting your heart to the Heavens. Affirm your oneness with Him by saying "I am one with God's light" or "I am one with the universe." It helps you feel protected and not alone. And finally, when you're about to enter a situation where you need extra strength and encour-agement, imagine a ray of light rushing through your body from above, filling you up, and illuminating you from the inside out. I like to do a variation on this when I'm driving in bad weather or traffic or racing to a meeting. I picture an approaching mist of white light blowing over me or my car as if by a strong wind. *Whoosh!* Just like that, God's powerful light makes me feel inspired, hopeful, and out of harm's reach.

Acting positive may sound like it can be an annoying or forced sacri-fice, but the gesture makes *you* feel good, too. Remember the *Friends* epi-sode where Phoebe sets out to do "a selfless good deed" though Joey swears they don't exist? Sure enough, she feels amazing with each positive effort. What Phoebe learns is what Spirit affirms every day—positivity is a give-and-take. It's tough to avoid the boost of happiness that comes from helping your elderly neighbor pull weeds when you see how happy it makes her. You can also do "selfless good deeds" for yourself and should treat yourself regularly. Take an extra Pilates class or cook yourself a delicious meal after the kids are in bed. Be good to yourself, or you'll have no energy to be good to others. No guilt allowed.

Positive contributions help the earth and universe thrive in a cosmic sense, too. Though Spirit wants us to be happy and succeed, they also need us to positively affect the physical functioning of the universe and heal the earth on an energetic level. The notion of positive energy fueling the universe makes me think of the movie *Monsters, Inc.*, where monsters live in a city called Monstropolis and provoke the screams of children to power it. Eventually, the monsters realize laughter is more powerful than fear, so they entertain kids as comedians instead. This causes abundant energy for the monster world. In our universe, you and I aren't so different from that furry blue monster and his one-eyed sidekick!

My Team broke our reality down for me in the simplest way they could. First, across a large map of the world, they laid a gridded pattern that represents its energy field. Then they added holes to the grid to represent pockets that carry negative energy derived from dark emotions like greed, pain, selfishness, hate, fear, power, doubt, and competitiveness, which damage the earth's and universe's energy. For instance, war-torn countries and crime-ridden cities whose chaos is fueled by negative incentives like greed, hatred, racism, and a lust for power have more negative pockets than, say, peaceful organic farmland in the Midwest. In light of this, we all have a responsibility to help "repair" the universe's holes by emanating positivity from our thoughts, prayers, and actions in the ways we've discussed. Doing your part to better our world is essential to this healing and the universe's flow. The good news is, I'm shown that nobody enters the earth in a negative state—it's learned, and because of that, it can be unlearned, too.

Spirit has shown me the earth and its energy field from space, vigorously pulsing when we exude positive energy and slowing down when we are negative. Other dimensions, including those on the Other Side, rely on this energy to exist. Our individual and collective vibration doesn't end when we die, either. When we move on to Heaven, we learn how to contribute to positive energy there and on earth if we come back for another lifetime.

In the end, a world full of light, bright energy is a win-win for you *and* the universe. Because Believe, Ask, and Act help you stay on your best path, learn lessons, grow your consciousness, and emanate positivity, your subsequent happiness both enriches your existence and heals God's creation. Your angels and spirit guides are ready to get started when you are. It's time you get to know them!

CHAPTER 3

Meet Your Universal Team

Your place in the universe is guided by your very own Universal Team of productive and enlightened angels and spirit guides (which I sometimes refer to with the collective term *guides*), departed loved ones, figures of faith, and other spiritual beings. Their job is to love, lead, and protect you as you dream and plan and remove obstacles along your soul's best path. Your angels and spirit guides are the movers and shakers behind Believe, Ask, and Act who act in conjunction with the universe's energy to make things happen. I just love talking about them.

Trusting and acting on your Team's guidance are what make or break happiness. I've noticed that clients who feel stuck when seeking growth or change lean solely on positive intentions, upbeat thoughts, and an established faith, which engages their Teams but doesn't move their desires forward. They expect God to take the wheel, when they should be asking Him and His emissaries for directions so they can drive their own car. When you don't tune in to your Team's abilities and interact accordingly, you remove yourself from the very process that generates results. As my own guides say, "Ask and you shall receive? Maybe. Ask and be guided? Always."

The more you use your Universal Team, the more you'll appreciate and rely on how precisely they know your soul and can communicate through your instincts. Savvy spirits are assigned to you for a reason—they have a sense of your optimal path and have your best intentions in mind. By following your Team's lead and listening to the intuitive hunches and feelings they prompt, you will return to your soul's basic instincts, the ones you were born with and that we all have as humans. Ideally, it's from this beautifully lit place that you'll live true to yourself and move God's best intentions forward. Your choices are what allow the energy around you to flow, and you will have the opportunity for greater happiness and connection when you are really tuning in to your Team. "You have the power to change your life, and it is not a journey you take alone," my guides say. "Strip away your layers and remind yourself of what you are at your very core. You are from pure energy with the strength of the universe not only walking beside you but living within you, too."

Engaging your Team allows your life to move at a purposeful clip, so I want you to understand who these souls are so that you can visualize and value their role in the three steps. In this chapter, I'll introduce you to God and the Spirit that guides you, explain what their purposes are and where they fit into the universal hierarchy, and suggest a cool way to interact with them. Because clients' Teams show up in readings all the time, I understand this aspect of Spirit and their intentions very well. I want you to feel comfortable with them, too, since your Team is your greatest ally and support as you move through life.

TEAM BASICS

Spirit guides, angels, and loved ones primarily compose your Universal Team, though certain religious figures, teachers, and other spiritual beings pop in and out as you need them. A lot of clients suspect that only God and maybe a guardian angel or two are looking out for them, and they're usually floored to learn there's a whole gang of spiritual oomph ready to help them find happiness. And let me tell you, your Team is an ambitious and eager lot. They inspire your thoughts, reassure and console you in times of need, and steer you away from danger when they can. They send reassuring signs, create opportunities, and offer clues to solutions that soothe your worries and lead to soul growth if you notice and follow them. They try to help you learn lessons efficiently through nudging, insight, and inspiration. As you read in the last chapter, your Team also tries to ensure that your gifts are grown and utilized so your soul lives true to its path. Angels and spirit guides don't need to be acknowledged, but they do appreciate gratitude—they earn it! And don't worry, you won't annoy them by asking for a lot of help. In fact, when we *don't* call on them, they twiddle their proverbial thumbs and get a little frustrated by how stubborn we seem. While writing this chapter, my Team said, "Wake them up! Wake them up! Tell them they have guides, and tell them to use us!"

Your Team's job is to have your back, and the more open you are to Spirit's presence and answers, the happier and more positive you'll feel in everything you do. I find that talking to my guidance directly, aloud or in my head, helps me to feel connected to them. You'll do this in the "Ask" portions in Part II of this book, but you don't have to limit how often you engage Spirit. Reach out for anything—safety on a plane, help taking a test, patience at the DMV, or simply companionship when you feel alone. When I quote my spirit guides and angels throughout this book, you'll notice that I refer to them as one voice ("my guides say . . . ") since this is how they spoke to me for our purposes. But when I channel Teams for clients, it's very clear as to who is passing on the message. When you connect during the three steps, you may hear from anyone on your Team, be it God, angels, spirit guides, religious figures, or loved ones.

No matter who's on your Team or how high their energy is, Spirit will only support and assist you, not do the work for you. It's up to you to act on Spirit's advice in a way that feels right. If you find you're struggling with negative thoughts, ask your guides to clear them from your mind. Your Team's guidance should always feel nonthreatening and gentle, help you without hurting others, and create the highest good for all concerned. Their perspective might be hard to accept at times, but it will never steer you wrong. God's emissaries know your most heartfelt desires and empathize with your challenges. They will always guide you in a positive, respectful, and compassionate way.

And again, please remember that all Spirit is pure light, and their physical image is influenced by your belief system. So if the way I describe a soul here or in upcoming chapters doesn't resonate with you, realize that Spirit reveals itself to me either through my belief system so I can interpret them or through the client's so he/she can recognize the souls. Put another way, Spirit dresses for the occasion and knows their audience! I've grown up believing that Jesus is white and Buddha is fat, so I see them that way. Similarly, if you feel monks wear robes, and your guide is a monk, guess what he'll have on? What matters isn't what your Team looks like but that you Believe and know they are with you—and no, this isn't so you can trick yourself into imagining their presence. It reinforces belief, which awakens your awareness of Spirit. It's like when I'm in a loud restaurant and don't notice the music until my husband tells me our favorite Springsteen song is playing. Suddenly I can hear the lyrics and melody so clearly, though I somehow couldn't before I was made aware of it and then tuned in myself. Belief tunes you into Spirit the same way.

YOUR HIGHER POWER: GOD

I refer to the universe's creator as God or a higher power, but God is known by many different titles depending on a person's belief system—Yahweh, Allah, Divine, Source, and others. Spirit says God doesn't have a favorite name; He just wants you to establish a belief system rooted in a higher power. I'm also shown that God isn't a singular being but an expansive energy, though I use a masculine pronoun when talking about God because it's the most common and relatable way. Like all souls in Heaven, God's energy doesn't have a gender. Now some angels and guides do feel more feminine, masculine, or androgynous to me, but I suspect this relates to how I interpret their qualities—a nurturing energy feels feminine, while a spirit with a direct, no-frills communication style feels masculine. As for your loved ones, they present themselves with human traits, like gender, so that you recognize and relate to them.

God is part of your Team, and while Spirit utilizes God's energy to do their work, you can call on God directly when you need Him. His energy is unlimited, powerful, and benevolent. It changes lives.

God created everything in the universe, which means God created you. Everything is made from God's own pure, brilliant, and positive energy and therefore embodies His peace, mind, goodness, and light. In this way, you're "made in His likeness." God doesn't literally look like you—human features, smart dresser. A part of God exists in your soul, which makes the greatness you seek within reach.

Spirit shows me that God is literally everywhere—yes, His energy exists at the highest level on the Other Side, but it is also simultaneously in our world, too. Think of God like a blazing, fiery sun. Just as we benefit from the sun's warmth at the same time as people all over the world do, God's energy spreads across all dimensions. When His light channels through Spirit and people with abilities like mine (which is why some call us light workers), you reap God's benefits. His light is what makes things happen!

God's hope for humanity might surprise you. I'm shown that He doesn't ask you to "worship" Him and definitely doesn't want you to fear Him. Rather, God hopes you will participate in a respectful and honest relationship, a partnership if you will, with Him and His emissaries. God wants you to live virtuously and with love. It's not about achieving perfection—none of your guides expects or desires for you to pursue flawlessness because that's not possible. He asks you to create, nurture, give to others, and pursue true happiness because it creates a positive environment that keeps the universe pulsing with superior energy and enriches your time here. God wants you to do good for others while doing good for yourself. In a lot of respects, God's priorities come to me in a way that sounds a lot like Buddhist virtues—to love and find peace within yourself and the earth, to practice kindness and wisdom, to feel appreciation for all you have and share your happiness with others. You're meant to use a gentle, selfless nature to serve and help all living beings.

During meditation, I like to bring myself to a meeting area where I sit with my guides to discuss my abilities, how I'm doing on my path, and where my work is headed. I visualize myself in a circular ancient temple with large marble pillars and no roof or walls—just open space above and around me. The sky is dark, purple, and glitters with stars. In the center are two chairs, and I sit in one and wait for my guide to sit in the other. Souls dressed in white mill about, and I'm told they're all the guides and beings I've come in contact with in the past.

Once when I intended to meet one of my guides in the temple, though, someone else arrived instead. A beautiful white light with a loose form appeared before me. Its energy was so calm, clear, and safe that I immediately believed the information coming through was from God's essence. Our exchange was reassuring and mission based. We talked a great deal about how I was meant to teach others about connecting to Spirit; I immediately understood what I was told. I was smiling ear to ear, like *I'm so listening* . . . I didn't question the message or struggle with whether I understood it correctly; I just accepted it, embraced it, and felt grateful for it. At the end of our conversation, the light shot up into the sky and that was it! My guides inferred that I was speaking to The Boss, and God's tone felt like the embodiment of Truth. I don't know how else to explain it.

GRACEFUL GUIDANCE: ANGELS

Angels are another category of guides that likely will walk with you. They respond to your call with finesse and a warm protection. They've been in Heaven since the beginning of time. I'm not an expert on the angelic realm, but I have channeled my share of archangels, guardian angels, and what I call worker bee angels. Guardian angels are always part of your Team, while additional angels intercede when they're needed. I'm always impressed with how quickly and productively all angels respond to a request—and with care, tenderness, and devotion, too. All angels help more than one person at a time.

When I channel angels, their energy is lighter, higher, and brighter than loved ones and most spirit guides because they're so close to God. I mostly see angels as traveling orbs, flashing white spheres, and silhouettes of light. I also see angelic colors that symbolize how the angel is helping the person I'm reading. For instance, blue angels offer protection, green angels bring healing, yellow angels represent divine guidance, and pink angels appear when a person is pursuing, receiving, or emanating love.

I was taught that archangels are God's highest-ranking angels. Archangels Michael, Raphael, and Gabriel frequently appear during my readings since a lot of my clients pray to them, so they like to step forward to offer reassurance and comfort. Archangel Michael appears with a giant wingspan and offers protection and strength. Raphael steps forward to represent healing for humans and animals. Gabriel arrives in the name of truth, respect, clarity, and the importance of listening to your inner voice. A lot of clients call on Gabriel to receive the wisdom to make decisions and confidence to act on those choices. He is one of God's closest messengers.

You also have a guardian angel that is with you from birth until death— it ushers you into the world and greets you when you cross over. You receive a new guardian angel with each life, depending on what your soul needs to grow; "Some of us get tough assignments," my guardian angel says with a wink. I guess even angels don't have it so easy all the time!

Nonspecific angels are pure white, and to me, they're worker bees on assignment. These celestial beings are often sent to intervene in a crisis either as spirits or in human form, although angels have never been human in our world. My client Charlie, who was in a car accident that nearly took his life, had an encounter that came up in a reading. Here, Spirit showed me his fear, a car spinning out of control, and then a presence in the vehicle that appeared to me as a protective white angelic light. When I mentioned this last part, Charlie's eyes practically popped out of their sockets. "I thought I felt someone in that car with me!" he said. Spirit told me that it wasn't Charlie's time to die, and so an angel stepped in to save his life.

Most angels don't have gender designations since they're nonphysical, but they do have personalities and roles that lean archetypally female or male. Even so, the angelic personas I've encountered aren't decidedly one or the other, as art history and certain religious texts would have you believe. Gabriel is actually said to personify both genders—nurturing, passionate, and gentle (feminine) and strong, supportive, and motivational (masculine). In the Old and New Testaments of the Bible, Koran, and Dead Sea Scrolls, Gabriel is depicted as male, and his energy feels very masculine to me, too; but in classical art, Gabriel is often female. And while the Archangel Cassiel is said to be masculine, to me this angel feels feminine, so I refer to Cassiel with the pronoun "she." When I first began channeling, I met Cassiel, who frequently came to me in meditation. She used to sit on my bed and reassure me that I was on the right spiritual path, which makes sense since Cassiel is known for watching over the cosmos.

MOTIVATED AND MISSION BASED: SPIRIT GUIDES

Spirit guides are souls that were once human and have evolved to such a level that they can direct us from the Other Side. As part of your Team, spirit guides can come from different realms, energy fields, and other galaxies and solar systems with the intention of restoring our planet to balance, positivity, and peace. I'm shown that you've interacted with your spirit guides in a worldly way—perhaps your guide was a mentor, friend, or loved one from a past life—and that you continue to help each other out in every lifetime. You have many spirit guides in your life—some permanent, others transient—depending on what your needs and challenges are. They guide you through periods of transition, and while they don't solve your problems or take them away, they present opportunities and help you navigate them. They encourage you to listen to your instincts, think positively, and pursue happiness to feed the universe's ongoing energy.

When I channel spirit guides, their presence is specific and purposeful. For instance, if I see a Native American medicine man during a reading, he wants you to know he's guiding you to physical or emotional healing. A Roman gladiator guide wants to help you pursue strength. The first guide I met for myself was an Egyptian who taught me how to interpret Spirit's messages. I've come to learn that spirit guides are culturally diverse and usually in a way that resonates with the person I'm reading. The guide's identity is from a life they once shared with the person they're guiding, and though you may not consciously remember this relationship, the soul's persona always feels comfortable or familiar. A spirit guide's life might have even existed in other dimensions, and these are the planetary guides I mentioned earlier. I'm shown they are on the same level of consciousness as angels but in different realms.

In addition to your guardian angel, I'm also shown that in each lifetime, you have a permanent and consistent guide that acts like a caseworker. This guide helps determine who your permanent and transient guides and angels are. This spirit might assign an angel for nurturing, a Native American to join you on a spiritual quest, and a figure of faith if you pray to that soul. A caseworker guide has been mortal and understands the human experience. I don't know if I've ever seen one, but Spirit tells me they exist.

HOLY MOLY: FIGURES OF FAITH

Healers, teachers, saints, and prophets who walked the earth can be part of your Team if you ask them to be or pray to them for a specific reason, but they aren't as common a force in most people's Teams as their angels and spirit guides. In some circles, these souls are called Ascended Masters. They include Jesus, Mother Mary, Ganesh, Buddha, Quan Yin, Mother Teresa, and Muhammad. These teachers are at one of the highest levels of consciousness, and while they're affiliated with certain faiths, people of *any* faith can call on them for healing, guidance, and support. I find that these figures can have symbolic significance for the person I'm reading—Mary, for example, offers female strength particularly to mothers. St. Joseph supports children, and St. Anthony shows up when a client is lost in life. Saints also feature when a person prays to them. I once read a woman named Janice who had a strong faith, and I saw that she fervently prayed the rosary. I wasn't at all surprised when a fleet of saints stood behind her and told me they're on her Team! Janice has an affection for these deities, so they're always with her.

WE ARE FAMILY: DEPARTED LOVED ONES

The souls of your departed loved ones are proud members of your Team. Loved ones address what's going on in the here and now, though they can't intervene or guide you on your soul path the way angels and spirit guides do. They offer comfort, give advice, offer warnings, and encourage happiness. They send signs and guidance related to love, protection, and reassurance. If you miss their presence and talk to them aloud or in your head, they can use their energy to help you feel them around you or direct your attention to a tangible symbol that reminds you of them like a butterfly, penny, feather, or song on the radio. These souls excel with human experiences, and it makes sense to consider their strengths in life when you call upon a departed loved one for guidance. If you need help self-reflecting and Mom was a therapist, call on her. If your late aunt once thrived despite a chronic disease and you need guidance about a health diagnosis, she could be your lady.

Loved ones are a natural fit for your Team because they're part of what's called your soul pack. A soul pack is a group of souls that are with you in every lifetime—close friends, family, and others who shape and care for you. Most people in your soul pack are here to offer happiness and support, but some stay connected to you to resolve unfinished business from a past life like relationships that need closure or forgiveness or lessons that still need to be learned like better communication, self-love, accountability, or love for others. Members of your living soul pack don't have to be permanent fixtures, either; they can drift in and out or mean a lot for a short time, but they always impact your life and imprint in some way.

Soul mates are part of a soul pack, and we all have a few; these can be partners, friends, or anyone else you're connected to in a meaningful way. Your role in the person's life can even be "contracted," or divinely agreed upon before incarnating, which I see a lot between spouses. My client Rachel takes care of her husband with ALS, and Spirit's shown me that she's been contracted to care for him in prior lives, too, but as his mother, brother, or sister. I learned that I also have a contract with my husband, Chris, that says if our other romances didn't work out, we'd meet up to spend the rest of our lives together, which is exactly what happened! For what it's worth, we think this is a pretty lame agreement, so I plan to renegotiate our deal between lives. I don't want to wait to find Chris in my next one!

INTO THE WILD: SPIRIT ANIMALS

I've channeled many pets in my career (dogs, cats, a horse . . .), but there are also symbolic spirit animals that can be part of your Team. Many faiths and cultures believe in spirit animals; for instance, Native Americans recognize animal spirit guides (also called animal totems), and Mayans believe that every person has an animal companion that shares their soul. Animal souls exist in a different sphere than where I channel from, unless they're with a departed loved one who calls on his or her deceased pet for company (deceased pets can't become guides). When animal guides appear during a reading, I share what I'm shown and ask clients to explore their meaning as homework.

In my experience, spirit animals are on Teams for clients who feel connected to the earth, relate to or practice a faith that the spirit animal comes from, and/or have a deep love for animals in general. My friend Steven loves to hike, and I always see a beautiful white spirit wolf behind him. Steven is really into Native American culture, so to him, this wolf represents protection and confidence. He wasn't the least bit surprised when an animal totem stepped forward during his reading! Neither is my client Barb when animal guides appear during her sessions. She is a regular Dr. Doolittle who volunteers at an animal shelter and has three dogs that she pampers like children. Barb also has a lot of trust and intimacy conflicts with humans due to an alcoholic father and abusive ex-husband, so animals represent loyalty and unconditional love to her in a way that she needs. Barb is always surrounded by owl spirits that represent wisdom, and a week before I last sat with her, I saw a huge, beautiful owl in a tree near my house! My guides made sure I saw it so that I could mention it to Barb as reassurance that her Team is all around her.

If you notice a recurring animal theme in your life, look into what the creature means and accept the first positive definition you read; consider the search itself a guided event from your Team. The Internet is full of surprisingly consistent interpretations of spirit animals, so you can safely begin there.

MEET MY UNIVERSAL TEAM

Like your Team, mine is purposeful, reliable, and always in flux and expanding. After I accepted my gift, my first guide was an Egyptian who explained that I was meant to teach others about Spirit and the afterlife and that various beings would help. I began seeing angels after that and a white-bearded man in a robe who'd attend meditations with Pat. There have also been Native Americans, Hindu monks, Tibetans, and Roman gladiators. Recently during meditation, I was brought to a conference room with at least two dozen guides—all white light beings—that I'm told are assigned to me and monitoring my path. I found it very comforting to know I'm looked after like that. Thankfully, Pat taught me how to "turn on and off" my gift, so I mostly see my guides when I'm doing a spiritual practice like prayer, channeling, or automatic writing. I always feel them around me, but I don't always communicate with them for the sake of balance—some of this is my doing and some theirs. When I take a vacation, for example, they go quiet and encourage me to commit to my other priorities like family, friends, and downtime.

I currently have two spirit guides and a feminine energy that I lean on regularly, though other spirit guides, angels, and departed loved ones transition in and out. In the middle of the night, my bedroom can feel like Grand Central Terminal; it's so full of commotion! It's not unusual for me to roll over, still half-asleep, to find my father-in-law, great-grandmother, and uncle standing at the foot of my bed. Once in a while I see a flash of a full apparition, but I typically feel the souls around me and at the same time hear or see their names in my third eye to identify them. And every morning, my guides wake me up with a sweet greeting—"Today you rise with bliss in your eyes"—which is just so chirpy and optimistic it starts every day with a smile.

One of my biggest guns is a planetary guide, who's a higher-level being that helps me grow my mediumship skills and faith in the universe. He's very cerebral and says things like "I want to expand the perimeters of the confined mind." Seriously, that's how he talks, and I'm sure it sounds wild coming from my mouth. He's very tall and protective, and during readings, I find myself looking up at him because he makes sure his presence is always larger than mine. He keeps me on message and is very calculated in his approach.

I also have a spirit guide who's an adorable Buddhist yogi who rings in on positivity, meditation, and being one with your soul. He wears a clay-colored robe, has a shiny bald head, and floats around in front of me with his legs crossed. He's all about knowledge and wisdom.

Finally, I have a feminine, higher-energy being that feels closest to God of all my guidance. She says she's part of "the universe's creation and continuum." I know I've worked with her in some capacity between lives. When I first met this peaceful spirit, she said, "I have been all things, seen all things, and am all things." Translation: This soul has risen through all levels of consciousness and walked every realm. If I need nurturing or reassurance, she channels in. She has a motherly feel, and she says that in many lifetimes, she's helped me become a strong woman. I feel she has been sent to me through God and reassures me that my purpose is very God-driven, which is comforting and important to me.

READY TO TALK TO YOUR TEAM?

I've had years to process these revelations, so for me to go on about past lives, higher consciousness, and souls from other dimensions is second nature. If this is news to you, however, that's okay! Your Universal Team, including your angels and guides, will ensure that you have your own unique and fulfilling experiences with them in no time.

I love to connect to my angels and guides through automatic writing, which Pat describes as "taking dictation from Spirit." This is one of the most gratifying ways to speak with them because their replies are immediate and tangible. You don't have to strain to hear Spirit, because they channel through you.

To automatic write, you start by sitting quietly, relaxing with a few deep breaths, and lighting a candle if it helps you to focus. State aloud or in your head that you only intend to work with your highest angels and guides to call in the most positive energy, and then say a short prayer asking them to protect you and allow only high-level energy to assist and guide your writing. If your writings sound negative or pushy, stop immediately and picture yourself in a bubble of God's white light. Ask your angels and guides to clear the room and start again.

When I do a writing, I like to put one question at the top of the page and then answer it with whatever comes to me from Spirit. The key is to relinquish control and write without "trying" or questioning the process. Let the words flow. Sentences might come in stops and starts, as rhymes, or as a list. Don't try to be creative or clever, and don't judge what comes out; Spirit will guide your response. You might feel butterflies, a sense of peace, or nothing at all. Just answer the question without any attachment to rules or expectations, and see what happens.

To get to know your Team, I'd like you to "interview" your guides with one question a day for a week using automatic writing. If Spirit's responses don't feel strong or compelling, that's okay. Try again the next day. Members of your Team might also address your questions in real life or reassure you that what you felt during meditation was "real." My friend Molly once asked her spirit guide what she should call her and wrote down "Rose." That afternoon, Molly noticed a bird land next to her favorite rosebush, and the next day, her mom told her a story about a coworker named Rosie. Spirit's validating signs left no room for doubt—"Rose" was everywhere. And once Molly "met" Rose, other signs from her became easier to notice, and she felt more comfortable connecting with her every day. Now that Rose had an identity and stated purpose in Molly's life, she felt safe, connected, and excited to continue their relationship. Trust that what you're writing is from your Team, say thanks, and reflect on their answers. Not everyone is a medium, but everyone *is* capable of writing in this format.

Ask your Team any questions you'd like—*Who are you? Where do you come from? What are you doing for me? What should I call you?*—and keep your writings in a box so you can reread them to remind yourself that God and your Universal Team are always with you. There will eventually come a time when you can see and feel your Team's impact and presence all around, and you won't need "proof" that they exist. I promise you, though, that you'll cherish these writings as you begin to practice Believe, Ask, and Act.

CHAPTER 4

Three Steps toward Enlightenment

In Part II of this book, you'll engage Believe, Ask, and Act to help you overcome common blocks, but to do this well, you must first understand why the three steps work and how to utilize them. In this chapter, I'll first explain when to use the three steps and the importance of achieving and maintaining balance and control throughout, and then dive into how to execute the steps when you encounter a challenge. What Believe, Ask, and Act ultimately teach you to do is create happiness and change by connecting to God's energy, recognizing opportunities, taking risks, staying positive, making informed choices, and becoming the person your soul knows you to be. In fact, the more you use the three steps, the faster, simpler, and more effective they become until they're an instinctual way of feeling, responding, and behaving. The steps are a regular practice, not a magic bullet. With repeated use, ease will follow.

Believe, Ask, and Act will connect you to the universe and set change in motion, especially when you feel stuck, challenged, or bumped off your path. *Believe* is about establishing and practicing a belief system that trusts that a divine, higher power is working in your favor. It also requires that you believe that a Universal Team of angels, spirit guides, and other beings are guiding, loving, and assisting you from the Other Side. *Ask* encourages you to pose questions to your Team/intuition and learn how to hear their answers. It's not about just any questions, though; I will teach you how to pose specific, action-oriented questions that will provide you with the information you need to either get on or stay on a guided path. This will not only give your Team the opportunity to share their wisdom with you but will also ensure that the advice you get is tapped into the energy of the universe. Finally, *Act* insists that you take guided next steps based on what you're shown. When your actions are based on your Team's direction, you demonstrate faith in God and strengthen your connection to Him because you're taking leaps of faith. No matter where you are in life, you can only benefit from making the universe's priorities your own.

When you focus on Believe, Ask, and Act in a concerted and balanced way, you unlock the universe's influence and open yourself up to guidance that will keep you on a positive, purposeful track or steer you back to one. Spirit compares humanity's journey to that of baby sea turtles that have emerged from their nests and travel en masse toward the water guided by the brightest light they can see, yet vulnerable to predators and threats along the way. Similarly, Spirit sets our souls free in infancy and encourages us to travel together through difficulties and toward our best futures. Our Universal Teams act as our bright lights, guiding us through danger and into potential. But only you can make sure that you are heading in the best direction. Nothing will scoop you up and carry you along.

HOW TO USE BELIEVE, ASK, AND ACT

Believe, Ask, and Act can be used to guide you in good times and bad, though most of my clients lean on the steps when they face roadblocks and challenges, so that will be our primary focus in this book. In fact, if I had to sum up my clients' most pressing question in a word, it would be "Why, MaryAnn?" *Why can't I sell my house? Why is my career stalled? Why aren't my angels listening? Why, why, why?*

When life feels upside down, there's usually a method to the universe's madness, even when the cause is out of Spirit's hands. Not everything is divinely orchestrated; your own free-will choices can back you into a corner, for instance, and sometimes happenstance will just throw you a curveball no matter how smoothly other things are going (file this under "life happens"). Some desires can become stalled because the end result involves Spirit's notion of "perfect timing" (as with family planning) or other people's free will that either slows down or speeds up an outcome (contract negotiations, home sales).

Interestingly, I've found that your Team can also create a block to redirect your attention to help align you with your path, assist you in reaching goals more effectively, or force you to reprioritize a bit. This is typically what causes the feeling of "swimming upstream"; it is the path of *most* resistance. I saw this happen with my client Celine, who's a talented writer and master at adapting her skills to various industries. Yet for almost two years she wanted to leave an understimulating job but couldn't find a new one; her phone hardly rang for interviews even after she sent her résumé all over town. During Celine's reading, her Team revealed that they were blocking Celine from a career change because it was more essential for her to first move on from an unhealthy relationship with a man who was wreaking havoc on her life—ruining friendships, crushing her self-image, distracting her from growth. Finding a great new job would temporarily bandage Celine's misery and defer what she *really* needed to do to begin to feel happy, which was address her relationship. So, her Team blocked her work efforts, hoping the stalemate would force her to see her greatest and most obvious obstacle to joy. They wanted her to rejigger her priorities since her existing ones were harmful.

So how can you use Believe, Ask, and Act to alter the course of things? Change typically comes from simply tweaking your beliefs, methods, and priorities. (The universe has a great appreciation for precision and process.) Perhaps you have a strong belief system but lean so hard on it that you rely more on prayer than the combination of prayer plus action. Or you place a request with God in a way that asks for miracles rather than strategic direction you can then enact. It's also possible that you repeat negative patterns because you overthink your next steps and ignore what your gut tells you. Or maybe you Believe, Ask, and Act a lot more than you realize but allow negative feelings like doubt and fear to redirect some of your intentions, which convolutes the process and muddies the result.

It's important to note that since each part of the mind, body, and soul trio relies on the others for stability, having just one area thrown out of balance with a negative factor can skew the entire equation. An unfortunate example is what happened to an acquaintance named Joann, when her brother Andrew died from a heart attack. Directly after, almost everyone in Joann's family became ill, which added to their depression and shook their faith in God ("What God would compound grief with illness?"). At thirty years old, Joann contracted shingles—a virus linked to having lowered immunity and stress—and her mom caught a fever of 103°F. Even Joann's father-in-law threw up for days! But when I heard this story, it made so much sense to me. When you're stressed and emotionally depleted, your body releases chemicals that prevent your immune system from working properly. Your fuzzy mind has trouble processing your feelings, and this further impedes your soul's ability to heal. The entire family's balance was thrown off during a vulnerable time. It reminds me of how a blanket can unravel after one loose yarn is pulled.

Spirit wants you to focus less on "Why is this happening?" and more on "How can I get past this mess?"—and Believe, Ask, and Act will guide you to that answer. As you become more attuned to each step of the process, the people and situations dropped in your path will feel deliberate and reassuring. You'll act on Spirit's tips and marvel at how they prompt you to take targeted next steps with results that are better than you expected. Your Team will feel like uplifting cheerleaders, rooting you on as you pursue a positive, satisfying existence.

CREATING AND MAINTAINING BALANCE AND CONTROL

The Believe, Ask, and Act steps create balance and control in your life, which is integral to happiness. Spirit describes balance as a mind, body, and soul equilibrium and control as having the knowledge and self-assurance to move ahead. Balance and control help you feel content, centered, and confident in all you do. They allow you to appreciate your blessings and feel good about your choices. They also exist on a relative scale, with ongoing room for improvement, so you don't have to feel perfectly stable or totally in command to benefit. Spirit says your mind, body, and soul are connected both within you and to a larger energy field. So when you remove blocks, feel and exude balance and control, and let your energy flow, you experience an *aaah* moment inside plus give off a positive vibe that benefits the entire universe.

So what does balance feel like? You enjoy being in the moment, and anything more feels like icing on the cake. You feel good in your body because you do all you can to nourish, strengthen, and sustain it. You are calm, have clarity about who you are, and instinctively know how to move through obstacles. You might daydream about what can be, but there's no panic about whether or when you'll arrive. You're aware that you're seated comfortably in the driver's seat of your life, appreciating the scenery as you cruise ahead. You're thankful for how your Team guides you every day. When you're in this state, my guides say, "A balanced soul exudes the pure, loving light you came from—God's energy."

Believe, Ask, and Act give you a positive sense of control, too. I realize control can have negative connotations—it is commonly associated with white-knuckle gripping of the people and activities in your life and can bring to mind everything from overly strict parents to eating disorders to oppressive bosses. But control doesn't have to make you or others feel restrained or trapped. *Lack* of control is what leads most frequently to fear, stress, and other negative emotions that block your flow. Being in control means you have the freedom to choose the very best opportunities and take exciting risks that make you feel wiser, happier, and more empowered. After all, God, in all His wisdom, gave us free will—in other words, He gave us control. That is an incredible and generous gift, and it's only negative when you misuse your free will to do harm to yourself and/or others.

By focusing on positive goals and using Believe, Ask, and Act during challenges, you will achieve balance and control, but you must also *maintain* it to trust, hear, and follow your Team's advice. Be careful not to accidentally work against your best efforts. Anxiety, obsession, frustration, or a constant questioning about whether the practice is "working" will hamper your progress. Remember, too, that you're spiritual *and* worldly. Your soul's best path won't reveal itself without some trial and error, and even when you pursue it as conscientiously as you can, happenstance can sometimes still get in the way. Because you're on this plane to live a human life, God gave you instincts and a Team to help you along; He did this precisely because He knew you'd need help balancing your spiritual and worldly selves. Spiritual circles love to repeat the quote "We're spiritual beings having a human experience" and insist that your identity as a soul takes precedence over what happens on this plane. But one isn't more important than the other. How can it be when human experience is the means to soul growth, which is largely determined by how you respond to worldly challenges? Live and learn using the three steps as a compass, always with balance and control, and you'll make the most of your time here. "Your life will flow easily like water, down the river, even through the rocks, still flowing, still flowing," my guides say.

The practice of Believe, Ask, and Act helps you feel and own the balance and control that are essential for a content and fulfilling life. Now let's move on to what each thoughtful step entails.

STEP 1: BELIEVE TO CONNECT

Establishing a belief system that's rooted in God—in other words, trusting that a higher power created and ensures the universe's continuum—is the first of the three steps, and it is imperative for the practice to work. There are many reasons for this. First, acknowledging that you trust in a higher power immediately connects you to the larger universe, energetically clicks you into your divine guidance, and readies your Team to work. You must also Believe in God and your Team so you have a clear vision of who is guiding you when you Ask for help. "Without knowing us," my guides say, "you're reaching for air." Finally, claiming and practicing a belief system makes you feel closer to and more aware of your most loving and authentic core. This is the soul God gave you. To know your purest essence is to know God.

Having a belief system also lays the foundation for a positive lifestyle. Can you strive for an honorable life on your own? Of course, but establishing a belief system helps you stick to the commitment. It offers written texts, a like-minded community, and organized activities that encourage you to practice positive values, spend time with those who share them, and do good for others. All of these efforts spread positivity, which, of course, affects all energy and your life in a boomerang-like fashion; these are both energetic and behavioral laws of the universe, as I explained in Chapter 2.

Before you execute the Believe step, you must establish and find fulfilling ways to regularly practice a positive belief system that's compatible with the three steps. You'll know a faith or practice qualifies if love is its central message. God wants you to be love, give love, and embrace the love that's offered to you. At the core of all faiths rooted in God is that He is love and expects you to embody this, too. Look for loving teachers who espouse positive values, wisdom, and guidance. Spend time with spiritual texts that support your beliefs and are built on love, and consider using them as guidelines, parables, and structure for life rather than hard-and-fast rules that defy interpretation. You might even feel most comfortable accepting only the central lessons of certain passages—that love, acceptance, light, and being made in God's image are key to existence. Spirit says that's all okay so long as you maintain loving intentions when you act on God's behalf. When you emanate love to the people and situations that need it, this process energizes you and feeds the earth. And because God and your Team are all about love, they will help you to love who you are, to pay it forward, and to create loving relationships, as well.

If it's taking time for you to embrace a faith or practice that feels comfortable to you, Spirit says you can set Believe's wheels in motion in other ways. First, you can take an initial step toward figuring out what your specific belief system is—read, research, talk to friends to find beliefs that resonate with you. You may also want to visit religious or spiritual facilities and groups in your area and meet with clergy or members who can talk to you about their community. This establishes your intention to have a belief system, and it's enough for now if you plan to earnestly continue your search and act on your discoveries. You can also state an intention to Believe aloud, in your mind, or in prayer. To do this, I channeled: "Begin with your arms outstretched, if just in your mind, and say or think, 'I Believe, and I'm ready to receive my Team's information.' You must feel a conviction that your life can exceed expectations and that Spirit will provide answers for you to Act on."

Belief is not a generic discovery—there are no one-size-fits-all steps that will help you feel close to God, your angels, guides, and other figures of faith. If I asked a practicing Buddhist or Jew to explain exactly how to feel drawn to their beliefs, I suspect they couldn't. It's so personal. Exploring belief is an intimate journey that evolves in your own time. In fact, it's part of your path to discover your beliefs in each lifetime by listening to your heart, following your instincts, and embracing what you feel is true. As I tell my kids, "You're learning one story. There are many stories out there, and when you find the one that's for you, you'll know." Spirit says that because each of us has a unique soul that comes from God, those who crave inner peace will find it through beliefs that speak to them. Committing to belief systems based on other people's views and experiences, on the other hand, can cause you to lose some of your soul's individuality and authenticity, which will obscure self-discovery and the ease with which you'll move through life. Trust yourself and which beliefs reflect how you want to live.

Spirit does say it can help to explore your beliefs in a place that makes you feel surrounded by an abundance of beauty, power, and majesty, because God is at the heart of it all. "Let your preconceived images go and allow your soul to be lifted into the *feeling* of a higher power," my Team says, "even if it's just the essence of something bigger than yourself. You will evolve from there." Perhaps sitting in meditation pose on the beach or talking to God on a hillside makes you aware of His energy in a visceral way. When you appreciate the physical world around you, it's hard not to admit that it came from a mighty source. I have a friend who once said while watching the sun set, "God is good. What a master artist." She sees God in beauty because beauty comes from Him. Maybe you're fascinated by a sky full of stars or a baby's smile that takes your breath away. Marvel at them and accept that they had a Creator. When you repeatedly feel pulled to a place or image that brings you comfort and safety, those subjective feelings reflect a soul-based connection to their origin. Returning to them brings you closer to God as well.

Similarly, practice your beliefs in an environment that makes you feel one with God's energy. This doesn't need to be a religious building; perhaps it's where you first felt His presence. I'll add, too, that connecting to God or sensing divinity in nature may feel more apparent than ever lately. There's a thin, invisible veil that exists between humanity and the Other Side, and Spirit says it's "thinning"—in other words, God is granting us closer access to the planes on which He and His spiritual beings exist. So when you sense an inexplicable peace and contentment during yoga or while going for a run that makes you think, *Is this what God feels like?*, it's happening because He and your angels and guides are nearer than ever. That sensation should and is intended to help awaken your spiritual beliefs and practices.

When you are ready to engage your Team, you must revisit your beliefs each time. I like to do this as a belief-related statement or affirmation. When you create these, the only guidelines Spirit has are that they begin with "I Believe," feel pure and honest, and flow from your soul. I'll give you some more specific ideas when we get to the "Your Turn" sections of Believe in Part II.

STEP 2: ASK AND BE GUIDED

The second phase, Ask, has many more layers and is more process driven. If Believe is the heart of the three steps, then Ask is the blood and veins that circulate guidance to its intended destination. Ask is about posing questions to your Team so they can lead you to your desires and intercede if you veer off course; it also entails the ability to sense, look, and listen for your Team's answers, signs, and opportunities. Once you place a request with your Team, you must trust they're on the case. You will not always get an instantaneous answer or recognize the answer right away if you're not looking and feeling for it. Give your Team some time to respond to you. Spirit says that faith is imperative throughout the Ask step—you won't get anywhere if you Ask and then secretly cling to worries or doubt that you're being heard.

There's a lot of power embedded in the Ask phase. Asking questions demonstrates a drive to move forward and a devotion to your journey that leads you to action. It acknowledges your Team's presence in a concrete way, which solidifies your soul connection and allows the energy to flow freely between you. It confirms your trust in a belief system, which energetically sharpens your intuition to hear answers more clearly. This step also shows God that you're interested in change, even if it's a challenging road.

When your intuition receives an answer, it will feel fleeting and happen in the blink of an eye (maybe faster!). Answers present as a word or two, an image in your mind, a gentle nudge toward what should happen next, or an emotional response. You might feel yes or no, turn left or right. Spirit comes in your *own* voice in the same way that you hear your own voice when a catchy song from the radio plays in your mind, except it isn't loud. It sounds and feels like a whisper or impression—subtle, natural, and easy to miss if you're not careful. Your instincts' speed may make them hard to trust and accept, but don't let that stop you. I'm shown that your instincts are *supposed* to arrive in a flash; you're meant to sense them, use them, and act in one smooth move. Intuition deals with issues going on at that time; your choices might affect the future, but they deal in the now to help you make a decision that moves you forward in life. Keep in mind that guidance isn't always a life-changing eureka moment either; it can be a hunch or suspicion that you secretly know to be true. No matter what, instinct should never feel stressful, dire, or foreboding, but Spirit will keep pestering you until you act on what they say.

Instincts also speak to you in the third person. Learning this was so helpful to me when I first figured out the difference between my imagination and my Team's guidance. Brief statements ("Call the doctor") or thoughts that sound like pep talks ("MaryAnn, knock it off" or "You know you can do this") are all intuitive. Your own mind, however, speaks in the first person ("I need to call Mom before Friday").

Listening to Spirit also means being aware of signs. These include meaningful coincidences or "synchronicity," song lyrics, chills, dreams, and tangible objects like pennies or feathers that offer reassurance in some way. (Loved ones use signs to say hello from Heaven, while your Team uses them to validate their presence or as an intuitive nudge.) Signs can also present as a friend's advice or a suggestion that makes you think, "I was just wondering about that!" Dreams are another kind of sign and can range from a clear visitation to a feeling that sticks with you after you wake up. The more you recognize what it feels and sounds like to notice and acknowledge signs, the more you'll strengthen your intuition and send Spirit a message that you're ready to do this faster and with more ease.

My favorite answers can take the form of stepping-stones, or opportunities that "feel right" when you encounter them, and when you follow them, lead in a helpful direction. If an opportunity is essential to growth or forward motion, Spirit will place the stepping-stone and then prompt your intuition with either a "yes, this" feeling or nervous excitement—a sense that any later than now would be too late. Stepping-stones usually occur through synchronistic events, circumstances, names, and recommendations that guide your next step. Serendipitous conversations are also key here; Spirit likes to use other people to communicate on their behalf, especially when you're ignoring your instincts. The subsequent route may feel smooth or round about, but if you're listening to guidance, you can trust there's a reason. Perhaps there are many stepping-stones with lessons tucked into each. Most of the decisions we make affect many people at once, so there may be well-timed lessons related to others, too. Patience and faith are essential.

When my client Annie was diagnosed with a rotator cuff injury, her Team quickly laid stepping-stones to the right doctor. First, she asked God and her departed mother to guide her to one who'd have the wisdom and insight to help her heal. The next day, Annie heard about two great surgeons—one through her son's coworker and another via her own friend. During a quiet moment in the car, Annie Asked her guides, "Should I see the DC or New York doctor?"—pausing between each option. She felt a peaceful flutter in her gut when she said DC, so she called the next day, and lo and behold, there was a cancellation for the following week. Annie was booked for surgery right away and felt confident about her choice.

So how do you know if your Team is communicating or if you're listening to your imagination? This is easier than you think, because all you have to remember is that Spirit has nothing to do with thoughts that start in your mind—particularly if they're worrisome. Mind thoughts can feel negative and insist on taking one road over another. The mind is loud, and its thoughts play on a loop; they're based in fear, doubt, or other opposing emotions. They can cause you to make excuses, jump to conclusions, and avoid what's good for you.

One of the best ways to recognize what your Team's guidance feels like is to reflect on it *after* it leads to a great place. Simply think back on how the process felt and make sure that the next time you navigate a challenge, it feels similar. The situations themselves don't have to relate to each other either. When my friend Jen began working with a new acupuncturist named Phyllis to help her rheumatoid arthritis, she wasn't sure if she'd like her. Yet during the consult, everything Phyllis said "felt right" to Jen, and in just a few months, she transformed my client's stiff claws into functioning hands. Cut to a year later when Jen set up interviews with contractors to renovate her bathroom. She paused to remember how she felt when she first met Phyllis—calm, assured, in line with her ideas—and tried to match that feeling during the contractor meetings. When Jen met a great prospect named Bob, his consult *felt* like the one she had with Phyllis, so she chose him for the project. Bob turned out to be an ideal fit, because her choice synced with her intuition.

Depending on the size of your challenge, you may need to Ask follow-up questions until you clear your roadblock. If this is the case, your steps, then, will become more like Believe, Ask, Act, Ask, Act, Ask, Act . . . until you reach the finish line. No matter how long this takes, adhere to the following "best practices" for Asking questions and listening to answers. If they sound or feel a bit complicated to start, don't worry. You'll soon realize that as you practice the three steps over and over, your technique will become increasingly easy, fast, and instinctual.

Best Practices for Asking Questions

Ask is a very clear and deliberate process: Ask a question (or in some cases, make a request) and receive an answer. But as with any official procedure, there are better ways to do this than others.

When you Ask your Team a question, you must first quiet yourself. Find an undistracted moment and plan to stay there for up to fifteen to twenty minutes. This can happen while meditating, praying, driving, taking a bubble bath—anywhere that fosters a clear mind. If wearing or holding an artifact like a rosary or crystal makes you feel connected and centered and puts you in the best mental place to feel a connection, definitely do that if you'd like, but this isn't necessary for the step to work.

Next, you must perform what's called a grounding and protection exercise. This tells Spirit you're ready to receive positive and protected messages from your angels and guides. I like to use one inspired by my teacher, Pat. If you want, you can do this exercise first thing in the morning so that your Ask questions are protected throughout the day; or if you're saving Believe, Ask, and Act for a certain time frame (like during an evening meditation or your lunch hour), you can protect yourself before you begin. If you find that your obstacle requires multiple Ask sessions, you must still do this every time.

To ground and protect yourself, sit in a chair with your feet on the ground and take three slow breaths—in through your nose for four counts and out through your mouth for four more. I then say the "Our Father" prayer, but if you prefer another prayer that aligns with your faith or beliefs, recite that instead. Next, imagine God's white light streaming through the top of your head and throughout your body, and releasing all negativity from your spiritual, mental, and physical being. Allow the light to push out through your feet and ground you to the earth like the roots of a tree, with three cords extending from your tailbone and feet. Then visualize all negativity leaving your body and entering the ground. While this energy is in the earth, imagine it transforming into positive white light, and then shoot that light back up into your body to fill, encase, and surround you.

Your next step is to establish a positive intention. Intentions prompt thoughts, feelings, and achievements. The types of questions you Ask and the energy and intentions behind those questions will encourage the pace, fluidity, and progression of Spirit's responses. I've channeled intention statements in the "Your Turn" portions of upcoming chapters in Part II, but to create your own, here are a few guidelines to remember: An intention statement requests guidance based on what you want the outcome to be. The energy behind your intentions—positive, negative, stagnant—helps determine whether you flow along your path or hit a wall. Realize, too, that stating an intention means nothing if you tape it to a mirror or just read it, expecting it to occur. Using forethought to create an intention is a commitment to carrying out future actions.

My guides use the words *pure* and *honest* a lot when talking about the Ask step. While your Team is around to help you and lift you up, they will not do so if your intentions, motivations, or desired outcomes aren't coming from a pure and honest place. Your Team must know that your questions are driven by love and self-understanding. Your desire should serve the greater good, and your motivation must feel true to your soul and the direction you want for your life. For example, if you'd like to make more money, a Spirit-approved motivation might be that you want to give to causes you care about or buy a new home for your expanding family. The type of intention that gets ignored or blocked might be more related to gaining material things for the sake of outpacing your neighbor's earning potential or establishing power over a rival.

Less obviously, a dishonest intention could be that you tell yourself you're asking for more money so you can buy a larger home for your expanding family, but in your heart, you pretty much know you'll blow it on clothes and gadgets. In this way, you're not being honest with yourself and Spirit, and the actions that stem from your intentions will not easily occur. This is why it is so important to have a clear understanding of your motivations before you set out to take the Ask step. You may not always realize the extent to which you are fooling yourself if you don't think this through first, so it's important to examine your own patterns and desires for a clear picture of what is driving you. Your desire needs to serve the greater good, and your motivation must feel true to your soul and the direction you want for your life.

Another way to determine if your intentions are pure and honest is to check yourself and make sure your desires aren't fed by negative emotions like ego, fear, and hesitation. We all experience these feelings sometimes, but you can't allow this energy to drive your requests and how you interpret Spirit's answers. To be on the safe side, Pat taught me to establish intentions with the words "Please guide this process for the good of all concerned"— it's an efficient catchall to use during the Ask process.

Finally, Ask your questions. If you need to Ask follow-up questions, you can Ask multiple questions in one sitting, pausing between them to receive an answer, or one at a time as they come to you. Remember, not all answers will be instantaneous, so if you don't sense an immediate response, just keep your eyes peeled for signs and symbols in the near future. Trust that your angels and guides are on the case.

Best Practices for Receiving Answers

Once you have Asked, you need to be able to recognize Spirit's response! An important part of the process is being open to receiving, sensing, and listening for your Team's answers that direct your next steps. As I mentioned earlier, the most effective way for Spirit to respond to questions is by (1) answering with a quick, quiet voice, image, or feeling that comes from your intuition and (2) using signs like dreams, song lyrics, other peoples' advice, and uncanny "coincidences" to validate your feelings, answer your questions outright, or show you an opportunity or next step. When your Team lays a series of opportunities in front of you, and you follow them like stepping-stones on a flagstone path, they'll lead you to where you need to be. Because Spirit knows our minds can overthink, misinterpret, or outright ignore their messages, they often play it safe by sending signs more than once and not relying on just one medium, such as a dream state, gut instinct, or song lyric. They keep messages short and clear to aid receptivity as well. "We're not trying to trick or test you," my guides say, "and we're not trying to make the process hard. We want you to wake up your innate abilities, and we're trying to find the best ways to use them."

You can Ask questions anytime and as often as you want, but try not to wait until you're in the thick of a crisis or despair; negative feelings can influence how you interpret Spirit's answers, and too many distractions could prevent you from being able to receive the answers they try to give. The more influence your mind has over what you sense, the more likely the message will be skewed. Plus, when you're down, your energy is low, so attempts at movement on your part will feel much harder than if you are asking from a preventive place. You'll feel confused and anxious, and the situation will feel chaotic or stalled, as if you're trudging through quicksand or floundering about and ultimately getting nowhere. You'll feel disconnected from your Team even though they're always accessible. Clearly, this is the opposite of what positive spiritual guidance feels like.

As you listen for answers, keep your options open and trust your Team's timing. Spirit's responses may arrive in the coming days, weeks, or even months depending on how much time you have to resolve an issue. Don't question or overanalyze them. If you need a quick answer about, say, a job prospect, you'll get a quick answer. But if you're reinventing your career, that may take more time. Spirit's notion of timing is different from ours, and the best opportunities may not be readily available.

Finally, express gratitude. Any time you Ask a question, thank your Team. I'm always fist-bumping my angels and spirit guides, saying, "Thanks, guys. Good job!" Genuine appreciation breathes light into you and is a positive action that helps the universe. Plus, it's just the polite thing to do!

Tips That Optimize Your Results

I'd like to share three valuable tips that can radically impact the ease with which you receive answers during Ask.

First, remember that you are Asking for *guidance* from your Team. Do not expect your angels and spirit guides to do the work for you. It's not Spirit's job to make things happen, but if you're open and willing to receive information, you will be shown how to make things happen yourself. You're meant to navigate life with Spirit's help, using your intuition to help you learn, grow, and make decisions.

If you're not sensing answers from Spirit, try Asking your question(s) differently. One alternative method is to use an if/then statement. Here, you'd Ask your Team, "If I do this, then . . ."—and whatever pops into your head is their answer. You can also Ask a question, present Spirit with two answers, then "feel" which resonates most. Because your intuition comes quickly and quietly, you never want to pose an open-ended question that requires a lot of explanation on Spirit's part. Let's say you're fighting with your sister. "What is my next step for reconciling with her?" is more efficient than "How can I improve our relationship?" Your specificity has a second purpose, too: boiling down your request to its very core.

Last, keep your expectations loose. This does not mean settle for less than you want. When you loosen your parameters a little bit, you give Spirit some wiggle room so they can provide what you need in the best way. Spirit uses the resources and potential situations available to them, their energy, and your willingness to sense and interpret their messages to guide you. Remember, too, that you're subject to other people's free will. Everything you do and desire touches other peoples' lives, and their lives do the same—to pine for only one outcome is unrealistic. By expanding your options, you're giving Spirit more room to answer in a way that's compatible with your lessons and soul path, plus those of others. Bottom line, don't be too surprised if your answer arrives in a different package than what you'd planned. For instance, your road to a better relationship with your sister may require painful talks about your childhood, sharing grievances and hurts, and a vow to appreciate each other as the people you are rather than the expectations you've always had. At that point, your relationship will flourish, but the initial process may not have felt like the immediately warm bond you'd imagined.

STEP 3: ACT AND YOU SHALL RECEIVE

Act is the final step and has both immediate and far-reaching implications for your happiness. At its simplest, Acting on instinct and signs means putting one foot in front of the other, staying aware of what feels good to your soul, and using those feelings to create results. But in its grandest sense, Act trains your soul for what's to come. When we die and our souls cross over, we'll be put to work on the Other Side as Spirit that helps others. So action matters not just in this lifetime but on a continuum as well.

You are largely responsible for seeking happiness and change, but how you achieve this is up to you; it is your responsibility to make the most of the opportunities your Team presents. Long climbs, flying leaps, baby shuffles—there's no set way to take a next step or pursue a goal, because Spirit may have a different route in mind each time. I don't want you to hypercontrol the process or passively react to it. You must trust and follow what you sense, evaluate how the steps make you feel as you reach them, and have confidence and faith in the end result. The pursuit is as important as the end result.

A lot of spiritualists say "let go" is the last step in placing a request with God or Spirit, but I see "let go" as an initial part of Acting. It's an emotional intention that drives motion. Letting go isn't about sitting still, throwing up your hands, and accepting any outcome that floats your way because you assume it's God's will. In fact, my guides tell me that the saying "let go and let God" is about letting go of the fear and doubts that weigh you down and pursuing the opportunities God places before you. A deep sense of trust puts you in the best position to pursue your best-case scenario with an open mind and optimism that great things are within your grasp.

As you Act, you must push all hesitations and fears from your mind, because they influence not only your thoughts and behaviors but also the language you use when talking about your next Act steps. Saying (to Spirit, friends, anyone who'll listen . . .) "I hope I'm not going to another pointless interview" does not help the energy flow in your favor. Instead, "I'm going on an interview that I hope will lead to the job I want" signals to the universe that your energy has positive and productive intentions and goals. Your Team honors positivity, and they will be more receptive to guiding you toward the result you desire.

With every action you take, be mindful of how the situation and all the dynamics therein—the people, advice, tone, and so on—make you feel. Any time you question your process, consider whether the situation makes you feel uncomfortably anxious or happily excited. If it's easier for you to formally ask Spirit "Is this situation good for me?" go right ahead. Keep in mind, too, that guidance is encouraging, so even if a path is extensive or bumpy or makes you work hard, you should always feel heartened to go on. Positive building blocks should never bring stress or make you feel uncomfortable at all.

In fact, Act should always, always, always feed positivity. At its simplest, you'll feel good moving forward; think about how accomplished, encouraged, and downright invincible you feel when you've just tackled a to-do list! All positivity is contagious, and the people around you absorb it like a sponge, which the universe appreciates. When my friend Bill landed a new job with a company that valued his natural gifts and motivated him to work hard in a way his previous post didn't, he felt so good about it that the week before starting, he joined a new gym, cleaned up his diet, and shopped for new clothes. "It's a little bit adorable," his wife told me, "like a kid getting ready for the first day of school. But best of all, his happiness has been good for our relationship!" We are open, emotional beings, so we ingest other peoples' influences if we allow it. Bill's example of unintentionally paying it forward to his wife and their marriage reminds me of how a flower's pollen can cross-pollinate when it's airborne or get carried by honeybees to other flowers. Spirit wants you to allow positivity to help you and others grow and blossom as well.

Taking deliberate, guided action is always a more direct path to your end goal than if you Act without Asking. Just because you're moving doesn't mean there's forward motion. My client Beth had a clunky relationship with her friend Leon, who was an angry, frustrated mess when he was going through a divorce. Beth did everything she could to keep Leon calm and stay on his good side—taking long-winded calls at midnight, rearranging her schedule to meet him for coffee, and listening to him complain about his ex, who was still Beth's friend. She even prayed for him and sent him positive thoughts. But all this effort amounted to very little; Leon didn't seem to be healing as a result of Beth's help, and the friendship drained her. She felt imbalanced because she gave more than she received. When we met, Beth explained that she thought all her actions would help Leon recover faster because he would feel loved and supported, but she was getting nowhere with Leon because it wasn't her responsibility to figure out how to take away his pain. I suggested that she use Believe, Ask, and Act to reflect, revisit her intentions, and Act on what her instincts said. Beth felt guided to begin establishing specific boundaries to protect herself—like no calls after 8:00 p.m. and no attacks on his ex—which simultaneously gave her more time to nurture herself and others who deserved it. She felt lighter and more optimistic, and she spent more time with her family, who appreciated her. Beth's relationship with Leon also improved. She had more mental energy to give him occasional advice now that she wasn't caught up in his negative spiral.

Now, Spirit doesn't promise that everything will be perfect once you begin to seek guidance on your next steps. It is still a trial-and-error process as you learn to interpret what your Team is suggesting. So what happens if you make a wrong turn during Act? Take in the lesson, and keep going. If you follow a sign, feeling, or stepping-stone that later doesn't feel right, stop and get out of where you are. Take next steps based on what you want to achieve, but don't forget what just happened, so that you can avoid the same issue in the future. Try to determine what your Team is teaching you, too. The lesson doesn't need to be a big one; perhaps it's just a reminder to have patience or appreciate your own willingness to take risks.

USING THE THREE STEPS TO OVERCOME OBSTACLES AND RELEASE BLOCKS

After counseling thousands of clients using Believe, Ask, and Act and the principles behind them, I've noticed that there are eight common blocks that consistently throw people off their best path that affect the mind, body, and soul. It's no coincidence that they revolve around spiritual priorities that we're meant to practice in every lifetime. Are these the only priorities God cares about? Of course not. But they do surface the most among those I counsel, so it's safe to deduce that they're far-reaching and crucial to know.

In Part II of *Believe, Ask, Act,* I will teach you how to use the three steps to overcome the challenges that arise when you've managed to neglect, in some way, one or more of these eight priorities. How you've done this isn't important for now—you're human and your journey is not designed to be perfect. What matters is that you revisit and learn from the priority, then get back on your spiritual path; the way to make this happen is via the three steps. By using Believe, Ask, and Act to clear a block and thus practice that value again, you create change and happiness. Even if you don't think you're challenged by, say, a love-related or grief-related block, it still benefits you to read all the chapters and do the "Your Turn" exercises in each. Spirit made sure they're full of messages that speak to the soul; absorbing their lessons will encourage growth and help balance your energy in a way you may not even realize you need.

After completing Part II, you'll be well on your way to using Believe, Ask, and Act in your everyday life. You'll lead with your soul and live each day with a sense of purpose. Let's get started!

PART II

USING
BELIEVE, ASK,
and ACT
TO RELEASE
BLOCKS

CHAPTER 5

Start with Love

Surrounding yourself with healthy relationships does more than add zip to a Friday night or expand your definition of family. Love reinforces your best self, feeds the existing love in your soul, and allows you to dole out even more love to others. This is of paramount importance—God wants you to give love, feel love, receive love, and be love. He hopes that in making the most of your time in this world, you will surround yourself with people who love and respect you and that you love, too. Love is an enormous spiritual priority because your soul was created from God's pure, unconditional love. Your angels and guides want to make sure that you always feel connected to and nurtured by His energy.

Spirit shows me that love-related blocks occur primarily when one of three things happen: You choose to be in harmful relationships (romantic, friendship, family, and otherwise), you don't love yourself, or both. Spirit has a lot to say to my love-blocked clients during their readings, and the through-line of their messages is this: If your own love-related choices aren't serving you well, your Team will not help them along because their job is to keep you on your soul's best path, which is always paved with positive, nourishing love. In fact, Spirit may create detours that prevent you from moving forward in bad relationships or bombard you with signs to redirect your attention rather than give you what you think you want. As this happens, you may worry that your Team is stopping you from finding love or feeling loved, or having the relationship with others or yourself that you crave—but they are actually trying to help you rejigger your priorities. The redirect can only happen, however, if you listen to and follow their guidance. After all, knowing what it is to experience healthy love is a necessary key to happiness—it informs your relationships, work, and a sense of purpose and meaning. So of course Spirit wants you to find a way to make love—for yourself, others, even the planet—integral to your everyday life.

The people you choose to spend time with play a large role in who you are, how balanced you feel, and the energy you receive and put back into the universe. If any relationship makes you feel bad, it creates a negative vibration; this warrants attention because it, in turn, harms your soul, interrupts your path, and damages the universe's energy. Now this doesn't mean other relationship concerns won't upset or ruffle you—like when marital bliss naturally ebbs and flows, in-laws drive you up the wall, or you're in a friendship rut—but the way you feel about these issues won't stall your growth or get in the way of life continuing apace. They don't warrant Spirit blocking your path to get your attention. Your Team's focus is on those who harm your capacity to love and grow your soul.

If a client is experiencing a love-related block, their Team begins by showing me that "the writing is on the wall," the symbol for which is a wall covered in spray-painted red graffiti. This sign tells me that you *know* you're in an unhealthy arrangement, and you're either trying to fix something that is permanently broken or turning the other cheek when you need to be making moves. Among my clients, this happens most often with toxic relationships, negative codependency, abusive relationships, and dysfunctional pairings that hold you back. Clients are rarely surprised when their Team calls them out, because they already feel depressed, stressed, confused, unsettled, or unfulfilled, and the reason they've likely come to see me is to help make sense of this relationship.

What's hard about releasing love-related blocks is that you gravitate to relationships that feel familiar. Dysfunction is an easy choice; even if it's bad for you, you know what to expect from the dynamic. It's unconditional love that's uncomfortable to those whose sessions involve my graffiti wall sign.

Relationship issues with another person are not just about romance; they can apply to any dynamic in which love and best wishes for each other

should be the motivating factor—friendships, partnerships, family relationships, and the like. When someone comes to me while dealing with this
kind of block, Spirit typically follows up the wall symbol with a second
round of symbols to help narrow down the problem and let me know who's
doing what. For example, my guides might show me an image of clipped
wings to illustrate that a person is holding you back from "spreading your
wings," or I might see a thumb pressing down on the client in my mind's
eye, meaning you're "under a person's thumb." They might also show me
a bouncing ball and put it in either the client's court or someone else's,
based on who's doing most of the work and is in control. What all these
symbols have in common, and what Spirit is most concerned with, is that
they demonstrate the degree to which you've known your relationship is a
problem. And then they initiate a conversation between you and your
Team about how to clear the negativity it's creating.

Spirit says you can use any relationship that has shown you true love as
your benchmark for what love should be. Soul-fulfilling love causes your
heart to be at peace without fear, worry, or concern attached to it. It's a
feeling that comes without tension about what will happen and why. At
the end of the day, no matter how your relationship ebbs and flows, this
love contributes to your overall comfort and joy. It can come from any
person—a friend, family member, neighbor—and happen at any age. You
don't need to be in a mature or sophisticated partnership to ignite a very
simple feeling. In fact, when I read my client Jocelyn, Spirit showed me
she was dating a man with a roaming eye. "You're in a relationship with a
guy you don't trust, and you wonder if he loves you," I channeled. "But
when your nephew shows you unconditional love, *that's* how you should
feel. You should desire that love from everyone. It's what you deserve and
what you put out."

The way you love others is very much based on your perception of love,
which is largely experiential. If you know what pure love feels like and how
transformative it can be, you can more accurately and effortlessly convey
that to others. If you don't love yourself, you will rely entirely on other
people to feed your soul. This allows others to determine how fulfilled you

feel in whatever way they see fit when in fact it is you who should be in control of the love you experience. When you let other people control how much love you experience, you'll collect fewer moments to inform your understanding of healthy and unhealthy love. You will never feel fully sated, because the soul needs genuine love from yourself and others to thrive. So many of my clients are anxious to fix a relationship with their spouse or parent, but they have to look inside first. Their Team tells them *they* need to be the reason they're happy and then allow the rest of their circle to enhance who they are and bring additional light into their lives.

The good news is that Spirit says having a loving relationship with yourself and those around you isn't the tall order you might suspect. Healthy bonds should make you feel content most of the time—they're never ideal, of course, but more often than not they leave you feeling enriched. Take it from Fred Rogers, of *Mister Rogers' Neighborhood*, who knew a little something about the people that you meet each day. He said, "Love isn't a state of perfect caring. It is an active verb." Love requires tweaking, finessing, and accepting who you are and what others have to offer. In this chapter, you'll learn where to find nourishing love and how to recognize and strengthen love once you've discovered it. It's a beautiful day to give, receive, and be love to the world.

Believe

- Believe that God gave you total responsibility for your life and the ability to recognize the love, closeness, and affection you need. When you demonstrate, feel, and/or are surrounded by love, this creates an energetic pink light or aura. I see this pink light a lot during readings; it reflects your purest essence. My feminine spirit guide also comes to me in a pink, almost scarlet, light, and she's all about love. "If people would just open their hearts, they'd understand that love is all around them," she tells me.

- Believe that love begins with divine give-and-take. God's loving energy forms the crux of your soul, and your Team lovingly guides you to make wise choices and release blocks. Accept their love, and practice a similar give-and-take with others.

- Believe that the love you exchange is limitless and unconditional, just as God loves you. I once had a philosophy teacher whose husband asked her, "How much do you love me?" She told me she refused to tell him because it would put a limit on her love. I thought that was so emotionally astute—spiritually, too. Spirit wants us to let our love flow freely, no keeping score or tit for tat allowed.

- Believe you're born with the ability to be pure and honest in your love. Consider what happens when you demonstrate love toward a partner, family member, or best friend—what you sense is palpable and real. If the love you feel is romantic, you might call it chemistry; if it's friendly, you might say it's magnetic; if you're in a relationship, you might say you're compatible. Spirit tells me that what you're really doing here is describing and naming the energy flow. We are all made from the same light, and so we all have a connection that ignites a veritable reaction.

- Believe that the best love you can give to others manifests itself in many directions to include compassion, selflessness, generosity, affection, kindness, grace, and goodwill. All are demonstrations of love. When a client is in a fight, Spirit often puts me in that person's shoes so I understand what they're feeling and why they're feeling it. But lately, Spirit has gone a step further and helped me understand why the offender acts the way he or she does, so that I can feel love when I'm reading this energy and spark love in the client. For instance, my client Judy was fighting with her sister-in-law Meg, whose energy felt out of control to me when I channeled it; I could actually feel Meg's resentment, jealousy, and irrational anger. Yet as I sensed these emotions, Spirit showed me that Meg acts the way she does because she's bipolar and her father was abusive.

Bringing this to Judy's attention helped her feel compassion, a generous perspective, and kindness toward her sister-in-law that she didn't feel before. Meg's condition didn't change Spirit's guidance for Judy, which encouraged her to proceed with caution because Meg hurts her; but it did trigger a more loving perspective that helped Judy let go of hate, so that she doesn't carry that negativity around.

- Believe that embodying and emanating God's love doesn't mean you have to accept other people's negativity. Give yourself permission to stand up for yourself and draw boundaries. This is a loving gesture toward yourself and shows others how to love you. And if you need a spiritual boost when you're upset, one of the most healing things you can do is to send loving energy toward the offender by picturing them encased in God's white light. It will put you and the other person at peace, even if they don't know why.

- Believe that you don't earn bonus points with God or the universe for announcing your love or acts that spring from love. Love should come from the soul; it should be selfless. You should feel an inner peace and gratitude for the love you feel and give to others.

- Believe that loving yourself and one another not only requires humility but intent to find the good. It's easy to love in the abstract or when everything's going your way. But if you express your love even when you're in disagreement with a person or situation, your soul's default mode will eventually become love. Through loving self-expression, you remain a loving person despite ugly situations happening around you. So if you're fighting with your family, this shouldn't stop you from expressing love and gratitude toward other things like having valuable friendships and the love of an animal. There is always room for love no matter what is going on in your life. What's more, when we feel vulnerable or at risk of getting hurt, it's often our instinct to pull away or to lash out before we become a victim. But that defensive maneuvering only creates more pain and closes you off at the very moment that you should be opening yourself up to the possibility for positive change. With practice, you can develop and strengthen your capacity to love in a way that overpowers everything else. Tolerance, as well, is a great manifestation of love.

- Believe that all faiths rooted in God should also be rooted in love; thus, all faiths rooted in God deserve acceptance and understanding. You don't have to be a Christian to agree with the popular Bible verse "Love is patient, love is kind; love does not envy or boast; it is not arrogant or rude. It does not insist on its own way; it is not irritable or resentful; it does not rejoice at wrongdoing but with the truth." Even if you aren't Jewish, you can see the value in the faith's tenets that ask you to love others as you love yourself and trust that the world depends on acts of loving-kindness. You can't argue with Buddhists who espouse that if your love causes clinging, confusion, neediness, or lust, or if it makes you lose your identity, that's not love. Hindus feel all life is to be loved, which is a belief we should all get behind. There's a lot to love about beliefs that value love, and God wants us to respect this. When you operate in the world with the genuine belief that the tenets of all pure and honest faith are good, your sense of connectedness to those around you will increase wildly.

- Believe that God loves you and wants you to feel loved. You deserve love because you were created from God's love. He's given every one of us the means to feel a satisfying, deep, and pure love. He makes love accessible to us; it's one of His many gifts. "There's someone for everyone" is a true expression, but your best love might not be romantic. The universe may offer you a friend, family member, or animal that gives you healthy love. God makes love available, but it is up to you to embrace it. God values your need to be loved so much that He also makes sure you're guided and nurtured by guides, angels, loved ones, and other souls that live and breathe love on the Other Side.

- Believe that in Heaven, there is *only* love. I once read a seventeen-year-old named Ken who saw me because he wanted to connect with his deceased grandfather. Immediately, the man's soul told me that Ken felt lonely and misunderstood and that Ken felt he was a disappointment to family and friends. He considered himself a "black sheep" and battled self-destructive behaviors, including drug addiction. "You feel so alone in your world," I said. Ken burst into tears, adding that his grandfather would never like the man he'd become. I explained to Ken that there is no disappointment, regret, or other negative worldly feelings on the Other Side. I told him that he should never feel alone because his grandfather's soul, Spirit, and God's light are always with him and that his grandfather is part of his Team, as one of his biggest cheerleaders. It revolutionized Ken's belief system to know he can call on any soul he needs for comfort, guidance, and support and they'd provide it with love. Ken's sadness lifted, and I could feel his soul's energy lighten, too.

Your Turn

Affirm your belief that you can overcome love-related blocks by thinking or saying, "I Believe I am loved and accepted by all souls that are meant to love me and protect me here and on the Other Side."

Ask

Reach out to your Universal Team on the Other Side when you need to feel love, but don't forget about the loved ones who are part of your living, breathing, human soul pack in this world. One of the reasons you're even part of a soul pack in each lifetime is so fellow souls can offer you warmth, care, camaraderie, and connection from one life to another. If you enter a relationship with a negative influence, learn from the experience; and if you need to, allow that person to move on so you can return to the soul group whose energy supports and is in sync with yours. And though you will always encounter negative influences on this plane, trust that in your lifetime, there are more people that you should connect with than avoid.

One of my favorite love block/soul pack stories is about my client Jan, a devout Catholic, who was not happy when her daughter Lindsey fell in love with another woman. Right away, Jan defaulted to fear, criticism, and emotional neglect—the opposite of what these two soul pack members were supposed to give each other. Jan worried that God frowned on Lindsey's love, that her parents in Heaven were crestfallen, and that Lindsey's relationship would cause everyone more heartache than good. Jan and I worked together for more than two years, and during that time, Jan's Team helped her understand that God wanted her to embrace her daughter, that He loves everyone, and that there is no judgment in Heaven from any soul.

As Jan practiced Ask, her questions transformed. She gradually evolved, letting go of preconceived judgments and shifting her intentions toward a more loving place. Jan went from wanting to Ask, *Why can't Lindsey be straight?* to *Is she going to be okay? Will she find love? Will she be a mom?* Once she was ready to listen to Spirit's guidance, Jan's Team was able to explain to her that her daughter was on her soul's best path to find real love and lead a fulfilling and meaningful life—*these* were God's greatest priorities for Lindsey. This adjusted Jan's belief system, and from there, she began to feel good about her daughter's relationship. She felt led to invite Lindsey and her girlfriend to dinner, welcoming her as family. The more Jan worked in accordance with her angels, the more open her mind, heart, and soul became. Jan's bond with Lindsey is now strong, and they are able to resume a supportive, reciprocal relationship, which is what soul packs are all about.

The most common choice, and potential misstep, that I see clients with love blocks make is that they repeat the same patterns in every love relationship they're in—whether it's with a spouse, family member, friend, what have you. To start thinking about where your love blocks are coming from, consider your prior relationships and how both the good and bad ones made you feel. Then, notice if there are any common themes. For instance, if you felt abandoned in the last three friendships you had, think back to when your Team may have been drawing your attention—through signs, conversations with others, gut instinct, and the like—to the fact that these were not healthy bonds. Do you sense similar relationships, patterns, or guidance in any of your friendships now? Keep these themes in mind as you pursue new friendships as well.

Your Turn

I'd like you to think of a challenging relationship that you suspect is blocking you right now, even if it's with yourself. If you don't feel you're in the middle of a love block, consider a relationship you either wish to improve or move on from. In all situations, you'll Ask Spirit the series of questions below.

Spirit suggests that you call on one of two souls for guidance here. Your first option is to reach out to an ancestral soul or couple on the Other Side whose ability to love others or themselves was admirable to you. As you do this, you may want to hold onto an item that, to you, represents their ability to love—maybe a piece of jewelry one gave to the other or a gift that person gave to you. You can also Ask for your primary guide to join you here, since this soul has an intimate knowledge of your imprint and soul group, plus where you have been and are headed on your path. If you feel that your relationship dilemma requires protection and/or healing, you can Ask Archangels Michael and Raphael to be with you as well.

When the writing is on the wall about a relationship, you've already spent too much time waffling, rationalizing, and making excuses for why you feel or act the way you do. So for this Ask, I channeled questions that all have definitive yes or no answers. If you feel

"Yes, but . . . " or "No, but . . . ," this is a clue that your mind is interfering with the process; take a breath and begin again. Healthy love does not come with qualifiers. If an answer prompts you to Ask a question that isn't listed below, as Ask often can, frame your follow-up in a similar format so those answers are limited to yes or no, too.

Take a moment to quiet, ground, and protect yourself, and then call on the soul you prefer and state this intention: "I will walk my true path without the negative influence of others, and I will accept and love the true essence of myself." Ask the questions below, listen for answers, and express gratitude for your guidance.

For a Relationship with Yourself

Am I ready to celebrate and love myself?

Am I ready to make myself a priority?

What is the first trait I'd like to work on that will help me love myself more?

What is my next step?

For a Relationship with Another Person

Does this relationship make me happy?

Do I feel fulfilled, appreciated, and loved?

Will I be able to give myself to this person without reservation?

Are good days and bad days directly linked to this person's kindness and attention?

Does this person deserve to stay in my soul pack?

Am I ignoring what I know to be true?

What is my next step?

Act

As you Act on the information you felt during Ask, you'll become more aware of how the people in your life demonstrate their love for you, what you need from them to feel whole, and what you can give others from that reserve. You'll also recognize the extent to which the people around you influence how you love yourself. Spirit wants your relationship with love to be generous, comfortable, and active. Don't become complacent about love, because it has the power to create immense positivity in you and others.

One way to make sure you're surrounded by the love you need is to occasionally review the relationships in your life and choose how to manage any misguided love or harmful influences around you. When my Team shows me a broom in sweeping motion, that's my sign for when a client needs to emotionally clean house. It's not easy to admit who's hurting you, though you'd be surprised at how tolerant you can become of backstabbers, takers, those who rain on your parade, friends who make you feel inadequate, jealous family members, neighbors who wish you ill . . . the list goes on. Their behavior may never feel "right" or fulfilling, but it does begin to feel normal. As you think about your relationships and create new ones, listen to your inner voice. It will tell you when to tread carefully—or perhaps it's *already* told you this a while ago, and you ignored it or thought you could deal. Guess what? It's time to remove your blinders and see all relationships for what they are and not what you want them to be.

When I asked Spirit for more specific direction on how to determine who stays and goes in your life—friends, peers, family members, and the like—they suggested a fun exercise: If you had to be stuck on an island with five people, who would they be? Who would make you feel good every day, and who would help you survive? Your journey on earth may not involve scavenging for food, water, and shelter, but it does involve emotional survival. Your top five picks, then, should be your go-to people for love and support—those who are capable of sharing the purest and most honest love with themselves, you, and the world as a whole. Think about how those people make you feel, and make that a new bar that other important relationships should have to meet. The more you give yourself permission to protect yourself first, the less dysfunction you'll tolerate. You'll also learn to sense unloving intentions a mile away.

When you're considering the negative influences in your life, Spirit says that those who project their negativity onto you are the ones to avoid. People who are negative toward themselves are more benign, as long as you know how to respond to them. I once read a woman at a group event whose husband was loving, kind, and good-hearted, but when he walked into a room, you could feel his heavy energy. He needed quiet, solitude, and darkness to decompress. Spirit told me he actually closes all the blinds in his house when he comes home from work every night, and his wife laughed because that *is* what he does! So while one could consider him a party pooper, he isn't a bad person and doesn't consciously project his heaviness onto others. More importantly, there is a deep, mutual love between the couple. Spirit suggested she simply ask herself, *Is this me or him?* each time she feels compelled to lighten his mood. If the answer is "him," she can choose to not internalize his behavior and stop ingesting what he puts out.

Choosing healthy relationships is important as is managing how you respond to those you can't choose (as with family); but you must actively work to feel your own love, too. I find that loving yourself is an ongoing and evolving process; it's one long Act that never ends. The goal is to work toward having the mind-set that you deserve all good things and that you have the capability to give your love to others. You'll then feel inclined to Act from that point of view. This might include gracefully accepting compliments when they're given to you, buying yourself a nice bottle of wine on a Friday night, or making a friend laugh when she's down in the dumps. It takes honesty, regular self-reflection, and maybe even therapy to see and appreciate who you are at your core and what you contribute to the world around you.

When Spirit asks clients to love themselves, they like to suggest that you write down your best qualities every evening—maybe you like how you performed during a presentation or brought your friend a cupcake for no reason. You can even read what you've written while looking at yourself in the mirror. "Find the good in yourself every day, and you will love yourself more," my guides say. "Everybody who comes into your life who also loves you will be a confirmation of who you know you are." Being able to love yourself also helps weed out unloving influences because when you're secure in how you feel about yourself, you won't tolerate others saying bad things about you, treating you poorly, or trying to bring you down.

When you Act to surround yourself with as much love as possible, you'll *feel* the difference. The energy that feeds and emanates from your soul will transform and make you feel lighter. Your relationships will feel balanced among those who celebrate your wins and are there for your losses. You will laugh more, trust more, and cry less. It's a universal law that when you limit and release negative energy from your life, it makes room for positive influences to enter. After a while, this won't even be a concerted effort. You'll flock to positive, loving situations with people of like mind, and Spirit will respond to this shift in your energy by arranging opportunities for you to find and meet them.

When I began dating my now-husband, Chris, I was amazed at how quickly his love encouraged my true self to shine. I felt feisty and desirable, and I demonstrated unconditional love toward everyone I encountered. I regularly thought, *Thank God I'm myself again.* You'll know the writing is no longer on the wall when it feels comfortable to be, receive, and give love. You will navigate hurdles with true and loving support because you will only make time for those who lift you up. You will feel spontaneous bursts of gratitude for worldly and divine sources of love, thanking God for your angels, family, and all the love in between. Best of all, you'll feel at home in who you are.

Your Turn

Your Act steps will be determined by what you sensed during Ask, but let's support your process with an exercise to further embrace love. Think, for a moment, about what you would feel like if you loved yourself more or loved another person differently, if that's your struggle. What would it take to fulfill you? Focus on what really matters— maybe a partner who supports you emotionally or knowing that past mistakes don't have to define how you see yourself. Write this person or yourself a letter, addressing what you want to feel from your bond and what you are willing to bring to the table. Don't send the letter, but do keep it in a safe place to remind yourself about the kind of love you need.

CHAPTER 6

Practice Authenticity

A desire to practice authenticity is a brave quest to know yourself better, welcome that evolution, and share who you are with others, even when it runs counter to what they feel or expect from you. It is about pursuing what your heart desires regardless of judgment or stigma and sticking up for yourself and what you care about. When you express your authentic self, you do this while listening to your soul and, thus, divine guidance, which urges you to radiate love and act with integrity. "A desire for authenticity is essential for the discovery of truth," my guides say, "and for finding fulfillment in life and making it more meaningful and comprehensible."

My client John is one of my favorite examples of a person who knew he was deserving of true fulfillment and living his most authentic life. Before John met his girlfriend, he was a silly, creative spirit who enjoyed taking pictures and casually showing them at small galleries and coffee shops around town. But the woman he was dating was more interested in his lucrative day job than she was in his art, and after a while he found himself playing the role of well-dressed arm candy. As John spent less time in his studio and more time at charity functions that made him feel like a phony, he began to doubt his God-given potential. In this way, John allowed his girlfriend to impact how he saw himself—and he felt deeply empty as a result because his soul's desires did not match his outer world. So a year into his relationship, John broke up with his girlfriend. Without her negative influence over his identity, he began to

Believe again in his inner voice and really explore his gifts in a new way. He finally took the leap to pursue his photography interests as a full-time career. John broadened his style, expanded his clientele, and built up his business. He's now a successful portrait photographer, known for a playful approach that's uniquely his own.

I find that most of my clients who don't pursue their most authentic selves are riddled with fear, doubt, and worry about judgment from others. They have become pleasers, are concerned they'll be ostracized for what they believe in or care about, and can't even imagine what a different way of life might look or feel like. Your most authentic self, however, is the truest reflection of your soul, and there is a part of you that will always recognize it. As a result, any thoughts, feelings, or behaviors that aren't genuine to who you are or what you value can create roadblocks and make it harder to navigate obstacles. It's only when your efforts match what feels right or authentic to you that the end result will create contentment.

No wonder Spirit says authenticity is linked to how often you self-reflect and how honest that conversation is. You can't travel your best path if you don't know what underscores and motivates your choices. During a session, a client's Team might show me a mirror with my own reflection in it and sing a few lines from Michael Jackson's "Man in the Mirror." This is my cue to suggest that you think about where your thoughts, feelings, and behaviors stem from; apply what you realize to the situation you're in; and then own what you learn.

Spirit is quick to call out clients who don't self-reflect or strive for authenticity, because ignoring this spiritual priority has far-reaching consequences. Their Team will show me how the person blames others for mishaps, circumvents honest discussions, offers meaningless apologies, or ignores the role their choices play during a struggle. These folks think they can hide who they are, but the rest of their life gives them away. They wrestle with their beliefs, feel depressed, have anger issues, and chase dysfunctional relationships. They inadvertently become blocked from happiness and a smooth energetic flow because they create an identity based on other people's perceptions, willful oblivion, denial, and/or a fear of owning who they are.

In the pursuit of authenticity, I typically ask clients to reflect in the midst of challenges, a little at a time, because anything more is a tall order. If you globalize your search—as in, *I will now meditate indefinitely to learn who I am in my soul*—you will try to tackle too much at once. But if self-reflection is a regular practice and authenticity is your motivator and goal, your momentum will naturally build toward progress. It's like how my friend Ali had a meticulously decorated home until her toddler learned to walk, jump, and color, which basically destroyed the house she adored. Since moving was financially unrealistic, Ali renovated her house, one small detail at a time, until one day she looked up and had, in fact, a new house entirely. Likewise, if you self-reflect on a situation-by-situation basis, you will recognize what needs to be fixed, improve upon these things, and discover an authentic nature that feels as good as new.

I find that it helps to regularly check in with yourself to make sure you're being true to who you are and what your goals are. For instance, if a situation is unfolding at work that you're uncomfortable with, ask yourself: *What role did I play here? Has it happened before, and what did I do to help resolve it?* Or if you're in a relationship rut that makes you feel sorry for yourself, think about how you could express your needs and standards more clearly. Your soul's imprint has an innate understanding of what is right and wrong for you, and reflection refamiliarizes you with it. It helps you gauge the extent to which you're being true to your soul. This is so essential because when you're feeling, thinking, and behaving authentically, the universe's energy flows more easily in your favor.

In this chapter, you'll learn to use Believe, Ask, and Act to self-reflect during a conflict, recognize and adjust your thoughts and behaviors toward authenticity, and apply this perspective to future situations. Even if you struggle with your past, no experience is wasted, because it can inform and redirect your later choices. When you understand your role in a challenge, you can understand its triggers and avoid conflicts ahead. You become increasingly open to seeing who you are and sharing it with others.

Believe

- Believe that you radiate the divine essence with which you were born. This comes from God's energy and lives within your soul. It gives you the strength to reflect and express yourself in good times and bad.

- Believe that when you reflect, you must talk to yourself with honesty because as with any relationship, the one you have with your soul grows from open communication. The self-reflection process is also meaningful because it allows you to revisit a moment, see what's positive and negative about it, and learn from the situation. Think about what makes you feel pain, happiness, strength, frustration, and anger, and you'll become clear on how to duplicate or avoid their causes. Spirit says we all respond to and act on emotion, so turn inward to unpack the feelings that influence you, until you operate from your most pure nature.

- Believe that your angels and guides will help you create a life that's compatible with your imprint when you're willing to be yourself. Spirit says everyone has positive opportunities available to them, no matter how hard their past or current life feels, but you must Believe in possibility and that happiness will come if your pursuits are authentic.

- Believe that when you seek who you are and realize your potential, the search may require careful evaluation, but the result will take your breath away. I once read about a scientist who studied seemingly bland grains of Hawaiian sand at a magnification power of up to 300 times under a microscope. As a result, he learned that this sand is actually remnants of tropical sea organisms that look like shiny gems in luminous shades of gold, pink, lilac, green, and blue. In a similar vein, you must Believe the authentic nature that God gave you is worth a closer look.

- Believe that when you're in tune with your soul and God's intentions, you aren't just happier in this world. You're able to hear your instincts and follow them more closely. You'll also understand others better and why they react to you the way they do. All of this helps you navigate your life and the lessons you must learn to grow your soul and eventually guide others from Heaven.

Your Turn

Affirm your belief that you can discover your authentic self by thinking or saying "I Believe God's light will illuminate my true self for all to see." Do this while picturing yourself standing still, with a bright light radiating from the inside out. This is what Spirit showed me while I was channeling the statement.

Ask

When you're up to your eyeballs in a challenge, turn to your Team to guide you through it in a way that draws on your authentic nature. They will grant you the strength to stand up for what you believe in. "It's within the admission [of who you truly are] that freedom comes," my guides say. During Ask, you'll focus on where your feelings come from and spend some time thinking about them. If taking an honest look at yourself prompts a negative emotion like shame, unworthiness, or fear, don't avoid those feelings; admit what they are and the reasons you feel the way you do. You don't want to hold on to that negativity and then internalize it. Instead, look in the mirror and say, "All is forgiven, all is okay," and imagine your angst attached to a dove; picture it flying off, far away from you.

One thing I love about the Ask step is that it immediately shifts your attention away from any self-criticism or external chaos and forces you to really tune in to your authentic inner voice. This isn't always easy, as I saw with one my clients named Kathy. Over the course of five years, Kathy was in a dangerous accident, spent time in an unfulfilling relationship, and faced financial issues from battling her ex for alimony and child support. As a result, she made uncharacteristic choices and ignored her gut because she'd gradually forgotten what matters to her during a difficult time. Most of her decisions, then, grew from fear of being alone, financial worry, and feeling overwhelmed with the recent hardships in her life. When I read Kathy, her Team said she was committed to a positive path but kept hitting roadblocks because she'd lost herself during an exhausting haul. What mattered most was how she was choosing to recover.

When clients feel insecure about who they are and aren't clear on what they need to feel happy, they initially tend to sense their Team's advice but then go on to ignore it. They're so accustomed to doubting themselves that they second-guess their instincts. This, too, was the case with Kathy. At one point, she'd lost her engagement ring and suspected this was her guides' way of suggesting she reconsider her relationship, yet Kathy didn't Act on the sign she intuited. Instead, she hunkered down in her rut because leaving her fiancé meant taking a chance on herself. During a reading with me, Kathy's Team actually told me that they did move the ring to get her attention and said that if she continued making fear-based choices instead of chasing solutions that resonated with her soul, she'd stay in her negative cycle. I suggested Kathy Ask some of the questions in this section the next time she was in a stressful situation and listen hard to what her gut was trying to tell her.

So a week later when the pipes burst in Kathy's house, flooding her basement, she was tempted to rail against the universe and Ask her Team to cut her a break. Instead, Kathy asked them how she was contributing to the situation, how she could use her best qualities to fix her situation, and what she could do to create change. Immediately, Kathy knew that she wasn't mad at God and was actually frustrated because the pipes cost a lot to fix, and her ex was behind on a house payment that could alleviate her situation. Kathy also admitted it wasn't entirely her ex's fault; she was also mad at *herself* for avoiding a confrontation with him until now. Spirit urged Kathy to voice her needs, and when she did, her ex wrote her that check. She stood up for herself and what she believed in, and the universe responded in kind.

Your Turn

In the name of authenticity, choose one ongoing conflict that shines a light on how you may be responding in a way that isn't true to your soul. Maybe you're holding a grudge against a friend when you know in your heart that you aren't an angry person and are letting ego and pride get in the way of your true feelings. Maybe you concede to a role in your family—breadwinner, caregiver, punching bag—that others put on you but doesn't reflect your desires. For three days in a row, do Meditations 1, 2, and 3 that I've channeled below. Ask each question according to the parameters and suggestions laid out in Chapter 4 for your best results.

Call on a soul that's encouraged you in the past and supported your self-esteem. This could be a departed loved one, teacher, religious figure, God's white light—any energy that represents authenticity, encouragement, and possibility to you. Remember, you can always call on your highest angels and guides if you prefer.

With your conflict in mind, take a few deep breaths to clear your head, and ground and protect yourself. Visualize that the soul you chose is with you now as you state this intention: "I will think, feel, and behave authentically as I resolve this struggle." Listen carefully for Spirit's answers, spoken through your intuition. Say thank you after the exercises and as you receive your Universal Team's guidance.

Meditation 1: Know Who You Are

How am I contributing to this situation, and do I like the person I'm being?

What triggers this (mad, sad, angry . . .) feeling in me?

Do I find myself in situations like this a lot?

Who am I in my soul instead?

Meditation 2: Improve Your Situation

Do I want to continue thinking, feeling, and behaving this way?

What can I do to change the outcome?

What is the lesson in this?

Meditation 3: Begin to Own the Result

Picture yourself in front of a mirror with your reflection staring
back. Visualize a word on your forehead that embodies what you
most dominantly feel about your situation. Ask the soul you
called on to replace that word with a positive feeling that you'd
like to embrace, one that reflects who you truly are. Finally Ask,
"What is the next step I can take that reflects my soul and the
highest good for everyone involved?"

Act

Your next steps will guide you to actively embrace your soul. You'll
feel unapologetic for the views you espouse and actions you take—not
entitled or more "right" than anyone else, but comfortable with your
perspective and encouraged to stay on that path. You won't hide from
those who challenge you, your own vulnerabilities, or any lingering
doubts you have about yourself. Because you know yourself, you'll live
with an eyes-wide-open awareness of what matters most.

As you Act from a more authentic place, your genuine spirit may
behave very different from another person's. This might sound obvious, but a lot of clients ask if there's one Spirit-approved version of
authenticity when individuality is the whole point. Your authenticity

might even surprise *you* by being more daring, compassionate, or even-keeled than you realized you could be in any consistent way. This is what's happened to me. I've come to learn that my true nature is kind and loyal but also has an independent, fierce edge. I'd forgotten this because I was so eager to please in my early twenties and first marriage. But I'm certain this kind but assertive person is "the real me" because I feel what I can only describe as peace and relief as I go about my day, behaving in a way that opens doors when I'm in sync with my soul. I'm no longer hiding who I am and changing my actions based on a mask or misperception. I'm being myself.

It's interesting to note that Spirit assures me if you don't Act authentically, your relationships will suffer most—personal, professional, casual, familial, you name it. If you don't know yourself, you'll choose friends and partners who disappoint you, but you won't know why. When things don't go the way you'd hoped, you'll point the finger at others rather than examine how you contribute to a relationship and alienate everyone in your midst. It will always be someone else's fault—from intimate friends to government institutions—because the onus will never be on you. You'll consistently hold others, and the truth, at arm's length because doing otherwise feels uncomfortable. This may lead to intimacy issues because you'll worry that when people get to know you, they won't like what they see.

When Spirit talks about a lack of authenticity causing relationship blocks, they point to my client Bryan, who was bullied in elementary school and allowed the memory of his tormentor to upset him into his early forties. Bryan blamed this person for why he rarely, as an adult, initiated new friendships, trusted strangers, or participated in social situations at work. Bryan also flinched if so much as a conversation, person, or movie reminded him of his past. So when his wife, Tina, jokingly called him a "big dummy" for not responding to an e-mail she sent, Bryan freaked out; unbeknownst to Tina, his bully called him that, too. Bryan's reaction startled them both, and he hated that he'd become upset at someone he loved and trusted. The incident forced Bryan to realize it was time to deal with his baggage because, while he could act skittish or insecure at times, this was not who he felt he was or wanted to show the world.

Bryan had to do quite a bit of self-reflection before he could Act. He Asked his Team questions that helped him realize that while he was bullied as a child, he was beating himself up as an adult. He learned that he fed his memories by allowing outdated fears to harm great relationships in real time. When he was ready to actively value himself, Bryan Asked his Team to guide him to Act. It occurred to him that if he found his bully on Facebook, the visual would help him see that his onetime foe wasn't so scary after all.

Sure enough, when Bryan spotted the bully's photo, the man looked nothing like the monster Bryan had created in his mind. "He seemed like such a nice, normal guy!" Bryan told me. "Once I saw that he wasn't the evil person I'd demonized all these years, I no longer had a valid excuse for why I couldn't be myself all the time." The reality check helped Bryan release the shame, fear, and embarrassment he'd felt for so long and start exploring who he is at his core—a warm, funny, and surprisingly outgoing guy. He has since become more comfortable in his own skin and spends time with new friends, has a less needy marriage, and even organizes drinks with colleagues. In other words, Bryan fully embraces his true self and is at his best because of it.

Your Turn

Though your Act steps are dictated by what you sense during Ask, I channeled an exercise that will help you remain accountable during your authentic pursuits. Spirit suggests that you make an Accountability Board that helps you commit to your feelings and the resolution you want.

To do this, draw a chart with four columns, and at the top, summarize the conflict you're working on in one sentence or phrase. As an example, let's use "Being a people-pleaser at work." You can also post a visual next to this statement if you'd like—maybe a picture from a magazine that crystallizes the conflict, such as a desk or stop sign—although this isn't necessary for the board to work. Then, in the first column, choose a word that encapsulates how the conflict makes you feel, and be specific. So if your boss asks you to stay late at the last minute when you have other plans, a word like *insignificant* or *powerless* is more precise than *angry*. In the second column, state a realistic emotional goal, which might be the opposite of how you're feeling—here, *respected* or *valued* is apt. In the third row, identify where your feelings are stemming from. So with your boss, it might be "Childhood insecurities. If I don't say 'yes,' then nobody will like me." Finally, in the fourth row, admit your role in the debacle. In this case, "I do give in every time I'm asked to do something, so I've set a precedent that it's okay."

After you've created your Accountability Board, walk away from it for twenty-four hours, and consider how it reinforces or inspires you to change your current actions in a positive way. Reflect on how to correct this authenticity issue. In the pleaser example, you may want to have a conversation with your boss about how you are happy to stay late on occasion but would like to be asked in advance.

CHAPTER 7

Embrace the Now

Personal reflection is an important way for you to get to know your soul, identify and work through lessons, and tune in to your gut instincts. But it is also essential that you don't spend *so* much time or energy thinking about the past that you become emotionally stuck in that time or on those memories. If you dwell in this headspace, you may become too distracted to recognize special moments happening around you and helpful opportunities in the works. And when legitimate concerns keep you up at night—tight finances, strained relationships, health concerns, and the like—Spirit wants you to find the good that's occurring in the now and look ahead. Remember, the ease and pleasure of your journey depend on positive forward intentions and motion.

This block is different from longing for the good old days of college or reflecting in a way that leads to understanding who you are and why you behave the way you do. What Spirit discourages, here, is staying glued to the past to the extent that you are no longer living in the present. Spirit advises against the emotional drive to look back, stay there, and not participate in the life continuing all around you. If clients are obsessed with the past, they constantly look over their shoulders, wonder "what if," and consider what could, should, or would have happened instead. In these cases, my guides—who love a good driving metaphor, if you haven't noticed—flash an image in my mind's eye of me ripping off a car's rearview mirror. "There's no point to looking back," they say. "Push the pedal that accelerates you forward. Do not hit the brake or slip into reverse."

Clients who cling to an upsetting past are usually held back by a feeling or situation that makes them feel indignation or regret; and whether they feel vexed at another person or themselves, they replay the situation over and over in their minds, wishing they could travel back in time for the perfect do-over. But regret serves no purpose: The past is already behind you, and feeling unsettled only bombs your thoughts and emotions in a way that fragments and contaminates your current life—you know, the one God wants you to value, appreciate, and experience to the fullest. At its simplest, this could play out as beating yourself up over the fact that you wish you'd put your house on the market sooner than you did, because now there's noisy construction in the neighborhood that's inhibiting the sale. The thing is, you didn't *know* there would be construction, so all your frustrated woulds, coulds, and shoulds serve no practical purpose. Plus, you can't control the construction. See where I'm going with this? Spirit says that in this and any situation where remorse takes the lead, your best solution is to respond to what you *can* change or adapt to in the moment—say, planting bushes to boost curb appeal—and accept the rest.

When I think of more emotionally heavy ramifications of holding on to the past, I'm reminded of my client Adam. Adam was an alcoholic during his daughter Elena's formative years and deeply regrets that he missed out on quality time with her that he won't ever get back. Adam mentally relives the mistakes he made, and that sorrow and frustration actually block him from enjoying his time with Elena now. When they went to Yankee Stadium together, Adam lamented that they didn't go to more games when she was young, and when he met Elena's fiancé at Thanksgiving, he flashed back to missing her prom because he was at a bar. Rather than being in the moment with Elena—listening to the roar of a crowd or watching Elena make eyes at her fiancé—Adam retreats to how life should have gone differently. And in doing so, he evades the present much like he did when Elena was young—only this time, he lets his past interfere with the bond that he could be strengthening with his newfound perspective. Adam is dodging his lesson and missing out on new memories that could make them both happy. I'm shown that when negative feelings like shame, self-pity, self-loathing, and regret stand in the way of appreciating your life and moving forward, they leave a mark on your soul. These themes will surface in other situations in this and future lives until you learn from them and practice what you know.

When you can't let go of an upsetting situation, the remaining impression can take on a life of its own. You might turn your wound into an ongoing drama by continuing to overanalyze it long after the fight ends. You might let the past alter your identity by internalizing the other person's judgment. You ultimately wage a war on your most authentic self, and it creates a break from your reality that makes you feel unhinged. My client Tracy is a frustrating example of this. She quit her glamorous job as a fashion stylist after fighting with a boss who belittled Tracy's skills and taste. And though Tracy received three job offers after she left, she turned them all down because, in the back of her mind, she worried that her former boss's insults were true and she didn't want to confront that possibility. Tracy believed the woman's negative hype and allowed it to derail her self-image, greater purpose, and soul's potential. As a result, Tracy remained unemployed for *three more years* and had to move in with her parents because she couldn't pay her rent. The last time I ran into Tracy, she told me that she settled for a sales job because she needed the insurance. Tracy was thrown completely off her path because she couldn't let go of the past.

What I love about Spirit's take on being in the now is that it's a bit distinct from what most mindfulness gurus teach. My Team agrees that the present is crucial, but they don't believe that the now is all there is (especially since your journey's greater purpose is to better your eternal soul). Instead, they want you to accept the present and look ahead with hope. In doing so, you leave anticipatory anxiety behind but keep your eyes peeled for great possibilities to bring happiness or helpful opportunities. There's no reason to lose your marbles over a future that's yet to occur, because you don't know what tomorrow holds—you only know what you *suspect or fear* it entails. Planning for tomorrow is a great way to spend your time, but worrying about it? Not so much. While I'm at it, doubling-up on negative emotions outside the present is also meaningless. When I know I have errands to run, I'm already overwhelmed, but thinking about how much I want to cry about it adds fuel to the fire. This causes a mad blaze—*I'm so harried, and I wish I weren't so harried!* Yet if you accept and respond to trials in the now, you'll react in a more manageable and exact way because you aren't juggling multiple crises at once.

When you embrace the now, you head into each day feeling anchored to your most relevant matters and give them your all. You address, satisfy, or savor whatever the immediate moment requires from you. Putting all else aside, you recognize what feels good and have the space to consider what that moment is contributing or missing. The past can't hold you back because you're too busy welcoming what's ahead. As my guides say, "When you live in the now, your thought process opens to any and all possibilities for your future."

Forgiving the past and engaging in the present has far-reaching benefits for your life and soul. In this chapter, I'll help you use the three steps to carry on from the past and embrace today.

Believe

- Believe that your past is not meant to define you, no matter what it is. God didn't create hard times to upset you, and He doesn't want any of your obstacles to permanently mark you. Rather, your higher power wants you to overcome, grow your soul, feed your happiness, and spread positive energy. To do this, you must Believe your future *can* be different from your past, and that it will actively and energetically change when you let go of psychic baggage. "Don't rely on the past to define you another minute," my guides say. "Trust in yourself and Spirit that you can build a new story right now."

- Believe that if upsetting past circumstances were out of your control, God didn't "make" these events happen. Most are happenstance or the nature of the plane we live on. Don't focus on what has happened and why, but on how to navigate your negative feelings or situation. Use your Team, in the now, to illuminate a brighter future. They cannot affect what is done; they can only influence what's yet to occur.

- Believe that if you don't release the past in favor of the now, you reduce your ability to hear and trust in God's voice and guidance. Don't let your concerns about the past affect your relationship with God and His emissaries today. Keep the faith. Your beliefs have not let you down. If you enter a negative, conflicted state, your energy thickens, which makes it harder to tease out your feelings and listen to your instincts. On this lower vibration, you're further away from your Team's intervention and support.

- Believe that God's there for you *in the present*; if you can hold on to this and call on your Team for support, they'll help you cope with life in the now. Though I'll discuss grief more deeply in Chapter 9, Believing in God's unwavering support is a challenge for clients who mourn so hard over a loved one's death that they turn from the belief system they once leaned on for strength and power their days with negative emotions that trap them in the past. When this happens, your Team encourages you to do what my client Maria instinctually did when she lost her daughter in a car accident. Right away, Spirit showed me that Maria used her beliefs to give the death context and called on God for support. This doesn't mean Maria wore rose-colored glasses when processing her child's passing. In fact, she still doesn't fully understand what happened or why, and she gets angry that her daughter's not with her. But Maria accepts the loss and hasn't lost faith. She knows this tragedy will follow her for the rest of her life but Believes she has to keep going because living in the past brings her down. Maria Believes her angels give her the strength to climb out of bed, get dressed, and continue with her life. She also Believes that they send her supportive confidants to lean on when she's feeling blue. "If you know your angels and guides send you opportunities for peace," my guides say, "your belief will carry you forward." Because Maria embraces her beliefs, Spirit presents circumstances to help her cope and heal.

Your Turn

Affirm your belief that you can live in the moment by thinking or saying, "I Believe that I can let go of the past, which does not define me. I embrace myself in the now, along with my journey, divinely guided and angelically given."

Ask

Spirit knows it isn't easy to let go of the memories and feelings that hold you back. You can't just push heavy thoughts out of your head or pretend to be optimistic when you're down—and there's no tricking your soul into playing along. Time also doesn't heal all wounds, at least not on its own. You have to do the work. If you don't make sense of what hurts, it's like ignoring an infection: Your symptoms will only compound and change shape. When it's time to move into the now, Ask helps you understand how your past affects you, how to embrace your current reality, and how to move forward with hope. This allows you to sort through the feelings and relationships that weigh on your mind, body, and soul.

As you work on this block, your Team may point you toward forgiveness—of others, of yourself—and I want to discuss this here so you don't reject it if Spirit suggests it while you're listening for answers. Toxic grievances from negative relationships or situations, in the past or present, that create or created resentment, hostility, guilt, shame, fear, and depression can warrant forgiveness; and Spirit says it will help you turn the page and feel settled if you can reconcile these. As far as I'm concerned, forgiveness is about you and your well-being. It helps you feel that positive sense of control we talked about in Chapter 4, so you can return to a balanced state. A lot of my clients who choose to forgive themselves take this step when they've decided they don't like how it feels to conceal, covet, or exude ugly feelings any longer. They begin to own who they were during the incidents that upset them, excavate the feelings that led them there, and reveal the person who feels good in the now. As my guides say, "Forgiving, figuring out the lesson, and not repeating it is when real change happens and your soul grows stronger. You become more open and clear about what motivates your physical experience."

When other people hurt you, Spirit still advocates for you to be the first to forgive because it frees you from waiting for an apology that may never come and, if it does, questioning if the person's intentions and words are sincere. Hoping a person who betrayed you will agree with your perspective or that one day you'll simply stop caring about their opinion is magical thinking. And while I encourage forgiveness for your own good, I'm not saying that nobody else matters to this process, because they certainly do. I just don't want you to wait for anyone else to begin your healing process for you. Spirit always wants you to be kind to those who betray you, but the way I see it, this is easier when you are in a good place yourself. Forgiveness must come from a pure and honest intention when it's time to communicate it.

My client Lena's story is such a wild tale of forgiveness that any time I'm tempted to hold a grudge or hold someone to a past infliction, I'm so inspired by her strength that I shut my trap! Lena has spent most of her life trying to reconcile traumatic childhood wounds in an effort to accept and love who she is now. Growing up, her family participated in satanic worship (yes, I just said that); her father, who's passed, was a high priest in their cult. This meant Lena witnessed and was the victim of many gruesome rituals. It nearly made my head spin when, during a reading, Lena's Team showed me an image of her as a child in a cramped space beneath a barn's floorboards, surrounded by animal carcasses. It was so scary that I actually thought Spirit was showing me a horror movie clip as a symbol; I never expected Lena to confirm that this *literally* happened to her at the hands of her grandmother no less!

Every day was a fight to reconcile the childhood that helped shape Lena and the beautiful person her soul knows her to be.

As an adult, Lena used avoidance tactics to cope with her past; she drank heavily, cut off ties with extended family, and stayed away from any kind of spiritual guidance because she couldn't get past what she was taught about the afterlife as a kid. When I met her a few years ago, Lena carried tremendous negative energy around and within her by no fault of her own. She had trouble feeling present in her current life and enjoying time with her husband and kids because she was constantly distracted by the shame and fear that plagued her memories. Lena sensed a darkness around her and feared she was inherently "evil" because of her upbringing. Without even knowing her full story, I could see with my naked eye that Lena was engulfed by a thick and murky energy. It looked dense and made my chest feel heavy. As an empath, I could hardly breathe in her presence. In fact, when I channeled her father, my guides wouldn't let his soul enter my office; they made him stand outside the door instead. (He actually rapped his long, overgrown nails on the wall, a habit he had while he was alive. It was incredibly creepy!)

During our sessions together, Spirit showed me that despite Lena's tragic past, her soul was most certainly not corrupt. She was a product of what happened to her, and her true nature craved purity and light. But Spirit couldn't just erase her memory and negative emotions; Lena had to make sense of her experiences for it to benefit her soul. I suggested we use Believe, Ask, and Act to help with this process.

When Lena and I invoked the Ask step, her Team—which was primarily comprised of angels and Native American spirit guides who offered strength, protection, and healing—was quick to respond to her call and offer guidance. They immediately showed me that Lena would benefit from forgiving her situation—not for her father's sake, but so Lena could feel in control of her pain and anger. I suggested Lena envision Archangel Michael enfolding her in his expansive, protective wings as she did this. Next, her Team recommended that during prayer or meditation, she envision white light coming from her and shining toward the circumstances that hurt her, represented by a series of words, images, or other symbols. For each one, she could say, "I forgive." This would help Lena exonerate specific situations that haunted her.

In future meditations on her own, Lena went on to Ask her angels and spirit guides to help her know a loving God, find professional support, and feel safe. She Asked to know what it is to feel more love than fear. She wanted to understand herself as a unique and kind individual— not as someone her parents raised her to be, but who she feels she is now and the core values she hopes to personify.

Slowly but surely, Lena made significant, impressive, and well-intentioned strides. She established a belief in a positive, higher power and regularly calls on Spirit for guidance and protection. She spends significant time with a spiritual teacher, who's helped her access balance and peace in her life. She digests her memories with a therapist; and not only is she sober, but she supports other recovering addicts, too. Lena's marriage is more peaceful, and she feels endless love for her children and grandchildren. Her siblings are still in denial about what happened to them, so they remain estranged, but Lena sends them love and has let go of the implied judgment that came with her choice to sever ties. She unearthed her most genuine self, accepted and forgave her past, and makes an effort to pay it forward. Negative energy can't touch her because she has raised her vibration and practices spiritual principles that cradle her in security.

Your Turn

To usher you into the now, I'd like you to focus on a past memory that you can't seem to shake because it evokes negative feelings. You might feel stress, regret, or an overall dismay with how you handled a situation and can't seem to let that go. It might bring you pain to remember it, but it doesn't have to.

You have a few options for guidance here, so please choose one that makes you feel safe, not judged, and comfortable expressing yourself.

Your first choice is a departed soul, like a family member you knew or heard about, that represents kindness and forgiveness to you—maybe they were especially sympathetic or someone *you* had to forgive at one point. If this doesn't resonate, call on a soul that supports your beliefs, be it a religious figure or spirit animal like a snake that symbolizes transformation and self-renewal. I like to call on Archangel Gabriel as an agent of God in situations like this.

I'd like you to Ask the following questions during two meditations spaced at least a day apart. If you don't sense immediate answers, continue to think about the questions and allow Spirit's answers to present themselves in the form of signs, opportunities, aha moments, and dreams. As with the Ask process in all chapters, pay attention to responses or themes that repeat—this signals a strong instinctual pull that might unlock further work for you to do. For example, if you can't let go of your father-in-law's hurtful criticism, your immediate work may be to forgive him and realize that his judgments mean nothing. But in reflecting more on this, you might also realize that it smacks of a constant need for approval, and you'd like to deal with that. Please address one issue at a time; and when it's resolved and you're ready to go deeper, use the same Ask questions to do so. Coming into the now is a lot like paring an apple until you reach its core—here, that core is your true identity and light.

To begin, take a few deep breaths to clear your mind and relax, ground and protect yourself, and Ask the soul you chose to join you. State the intention, "I accept my past, ask for the answers to my healing, and celebrate the now." Ask the questions below, stay open to your Team's answers, and don't forget to express gratitude after the exercise and as you receive guidance.

Meditation 1

Why do I keep returning to this memory, place, or moment?

Do I need to forgive a person or situation to move on? If so, how can I do this?

What's missing from my now because I haven't moved on? Am I overlooking a void that needs to be filled?

What good can I take from this memory and apply to my life now? What should I leave behind?

Do I hold on to the past a lot? If so, why is this so appealing?

Meditation 2

How would I feel if I let go and moved forward?

What's the best that could happen?

What's the lesson in this?

What is my next step?

Act

As you begin to live more in the now, Spirit says, "You become more open to, and aware of, the wonders around you." Even when you're in a crummy mood, the first thing you notice isn't that life is horrible, discouraging, and a waste of time. It's how many great things happen in your midst that you rarely acknowledge! Suddenly a parent's hug can warm your entire body, or a stranger's smile can make you feel connected to a greater consciousness. It's invigorating to occupy your body, mind, and soul this way.

Consider my friend Diana, who couldn't afford to keep her small ad agency open when her two biggest clients took their business in-house. Diana indulged her sadness and self-pity for months before admitting it was time to Act on divine help. When she called on her Universal Team for guidance, she sensed that moving to a less expensive apartment and nesting on weekends would offer the financial and mental relief she needed until she could reopen her business. But Diana didn't immediately Act because her ego didn't want to scale back; she loved her extravagant lifestyle and brainstormed a hundred ways to keep it. Then one morning during meditation, Diana had an aha moment so strong that she felt like her guides were shouting at her. Diana realized that she'd spent too much time wondering how to re-create her past instead of creating her life from where it was at that moment and with hope for a bright future.

During Act, Diana felt led to search online for a new apartment, and on her way to see the space, everything around her looked different. Her perspective had shifted. It was the craziest thing—strangers on the street seemed more animated, the trees seemed to be a more vibrant green, and Diana's situation felt more like an opportunity than an albatross. By the time she arrived at the apartment, she was more receptive to the smaller space. Its breakfast nook felt quaint and not cramped as Diana had expected, and she noticed that the apartment had more closets than her current one. Diana signed a lease and continued to save money, and shortly after, her friend introduced her to an entertainment exec who hired her to do a marketing project. Next, she signed a shampoo client. The last time I read Diana, she'd chosen not to reopen her business but save the money from her freelance work so she could take a year to write a book. Like many of my clients, the minute Diana stepped into the now, she became excited about tomorrow and doors flew open.

You'll know you're Acting in the now when, like Diana experienced, life *feels* different when you're present. It's as if you've popped your head out of the sand, and you're exploring the world for the first time. You can almost hear your soul say, "Hey, there you are! I was wondering what happened to you!" You may even "meet" aspects of yourself that you've neglected. You give yourself to the people and responsibilities around you because you no longer split your attention between the past and present.

Acting on the desire to forgive feels surprisingly simple, too. This gesture comes in many shapes and sizes, including a live conversation, a letter, or an e-mail. You don't have to make a big display of forgiving, but this does need to be an action, not a passing thought. It's perfectly fine to forgive yourself, a situation, or another person in your mind or during meditation, too. Just say or think "I forgive you"—with no qualifiers. "I forgive you, but I hope you have a miserable life" is not what you're going for here.

When you live in the now, you will no longer experience blocks related to the burdens that you refuse to release. When I read my friend Carol, I could feel her extremely strong attachment to her friend Sid. From a spiritual perspective, I understood why: These two had a soul connection from many past lives, but in this one, Sid's free will caused Carol a lot of anguish. Though their relationship began as compatible buddies who completed each other's sentences and had each other's backs, two years into their bond, Sid began to show his true colors to Carol as a manipulative, punitive, and outright deceitful human being. As Sid became more aggressive and self-destructive, Spirit told Carol to hold him at arm's length. Yet Carol refused to listen because she wanted to help Sid become the person "he once was." What Carol couldn't see was that Sid had *always* been imbalanced, but he'd just stopped hiding it.

For almost a year more, Carol tried to relive and re-create their past rather than admit what their relationship had become. This created blocks for her. Some were her own doing, like the marital problems she faced when she refused to give up on Sid, but I'm shown the universe blocked her as well. Work projects stalled; she had a small fire in her house when she was out with a friend, bemoaning Sid's duplicity over coffee. Carol energetically fed these negative situations by acting against her better instincts, and Spirit said her guides also used these events to get her attention. They wanted to pull her focus back to where it needed to be—at her business, which had become second fiddle to her friendship, and her home life, because she'd emotionally abandoned it for so long. When Carol finally Asked for help, her life fell into place. During Act, she stopped talking to Sid and saw a marriage counselor with her husband. She also pursued investors to expand her company. Yet I knew she'd truly healed when Carol posted a quote on her Facebook page that was a reflection on the Sid situation. It said, "Your perception of me is a reflection of you. My reaction to you is an awareness of me." Such powerful self-acceptance can exist only when you embrace where you've been, who you are now, and what tomorrow holds.

Your Turn

Your Act steps will be determined by what you felt during Ask, but I've channeled five strategies that will help cement you to the present anytime your mind begins drifting to the past. Three are mental, since hindering thoughts can sneak up on you at work or in the middle of the night, and two are more physical to break your concentration in an actionable way. The goal of both types is to short-circuit your thoughts and feelings about the past and ground you in the present.

Mental Strategies

- The next time you start to think about the past, close your eyes and imagine the scenario on a movie screen in front of you. Watch it play out, and when you get to the end, replace troubled feelings and "what-ifs" with a positive conclusion. For instance, my client Lisa kept replaying a nasty argument that she'd had with her ex-boyfriend, who insisted on keeping their dog after they broke up. Lisa was upset because she wanted to have a civil relationship with her ex and reclaim her dog without any hard feelings. She visualized the initial argument, and at the end of it, rather than leaving in a huff, she, her ex, and their dog shared a group hug. This exercise encouraged Lisa to reconcile with her ex and create a "visitation rights" schedule with their pet. You, too, should plan to Act on your finale, so don't just come up with a fantastical one for kicks. Spirit says this will secure a supportive and constructive "end scene" to work toward. When you create and achieve a satisfying conclusion on your own terms, it leads to closure.

- Say a prayer as a positive, quick effort that helps refocus your attention. You can come up with it yourself, it can be a go-to prayer from your faith, or you can use this one I channeled: "Dear God, thank You for removing this negative memory, and help me appreciate the beauty, strength, and magnitude of your gifts that surround me every day. I also call on my highest angels and guides to help. Amen."

- Think of three awesome actions you could take if you used your energy to pursue them rather than dwell on the past. The next time you're tempted to sulk, you'll do one of these instead. The only rule is that the activity must create a positive outcome for you or others. So, for instance, rather than stew over the eleven doctors who misdiagnosed your health condition, write down how you'd use the time you'd spend on those complaints and feelings to write a blog educating others on what you've learned, take a yoga class to relax and center your energy, or play a game of Scrabble with the family to remind yourself that love matters most.

Physical Strategies

- Leave your space to do a distracting activity that excites your senses. Go for a run while listening to your favorite podcast. Take the scenic route on your way to the dog park. Sign up for an art class that demands your focus. Savor the moment, being mindful of all you see, taste, smell, touch, and hear.

- Find a reason to laugh. This doesn't have to last for hours; it just needs to change your mental channel. Watch *Tonight Show* skits on YouTube or call a friend who makes you howl. I like to send my daughter serious texts using the Crazy Video Helium Booth app, which gives me bug-eyes and a squeaky voice—this *cracks us up*. Laughter shifts your energy, raising your vibration and lightening your perspective.

CHAPTER 8

Move Past
Doubt and Fear

D oubt and fear are like the Bonnie and Clyde of the universe—
spiritual outlaws gunning to raid your soul and rob it blind of
happiness if you let them. If you're limiting your potential in any
way, there's a fine chance your hesitations are underscored by these partners in crime. They are the source of most negativity, and Spirit says that
overcoming them is a major lesson we must learn in each lifetime. Doubt
and fear will hold you back from being your best, and when that happens,
you set yourself up for shame and regret—two of the heaviest burdens your
soul can carry and that flatten your growth.

So what do most of my clients doubt and fear? More like, what *don't*
they? I've come to believe that if you can feel it, you can doubt or fear it.
Rejection, intimacy, abandonment, humiliation, judgment, loneliness,
embarrassment, ridicule, not living up to your potential, expressing yourself, *not* expressing yourself—these are the biggies. Doubt and fear can
provoke a momentary distress over the unknown or a long-term worry that
you'll fail or disappoint yourself or others. The feelings of dread and suspicion that they breed can become so familiar that they persuade people to
stop taking bold risks. The truth is, they're all mind games, and we are all
susceptible. When doubt and fear block a client, Spirit calls it like it
is—"Doubt and fear, MaryAnn . . . " As in *Here we go again . . .*

When Spirit mentions that a client wrestles with a doubt and fear block,
they're usually referring to one of two scenarios: a situational reaction or

one that's crippling and continuous, both of which stop you from making positive choices that help you move forward. Situational fear is what you feel when you're in a dubious position—say, you lost your job and worry about making mortgage payments, or your loved one is ill in the hospital and you fear he might die. Here, the feeling passes when the circumstance does. This type of doubt and fear is part of life, and no matter how many times you manage it in one scenario, it will resurface in others. Spirit says it's an ongoing obstacle, but you'll handle it better each time since you've been there before.

Spirit's second category is an ongoing, chronic anxiety that influences every aspect of your life—the relationships, thoughts, beliefs, and daily events that feel impossible to navigate because they're darkened by a bleak undercurrent of doubt and fear. This is a constant hesitation in your mind that makes you think *I don't know about that . . .* , often because you have trouble with trust and change. Spirit says chronic fear and doubt are debilitating; they don't create a bump in the road that you'll encounter, conquer, and move on from but rather manifest as a relentless foreboding that everything you touch will turn to pot. When this type of doubt and fear interferes, Spirit shows me Superman's phone booth because Clark Kent enters it bumbling and afraid but emerges valiant! This is your future, too, when you overcome doubt and fear.

It's important to realize that exercising doubt and fear is not the same as exercising caution or prudent thinking. I understand that when you feel nervous, hopeless, and out of control, you don't want to trust the world outside yourself, but you must try. I have a friend named Mattie who doesn't like the queasy stomach and mental gymnastics that come with feeling afraid or uncertain, so she makes fear- and doubt-based choices that protect her from her fear- and doubt-based feelings! For example, she repeatedly doubts her doctors and will skip appointments or not follow through with the tests they suggest. Mattie tells herself it's because she knows her body better than the experts, but what's really happening is that she doesn't trust that her Team will guide her, is afraid of a diagnosis that could force her to change in some way, and doubts that she'll have the time or energy to help herself once she's given a treatment plan. She tells herself she's just being careful, judicious, and self-protective, but she's really demonstrating a lack of trust—in herself, in others, and God, too. It's ironic—Mattie's basically afraid of her own fear. Defaulting to inertia on the other hand? Well, that's easy, comfortable, and safe.

Spirit says the telltale sign that you are acting from fear and not caution is that caution never stops you from forward motion. It's a fleeting impulse that helps you make productive decisions—should I invest my money, take this job, go on that date—not freeze you in place because all you can imagine are impossible outcomes. And as you might guess, caution is often instinctual, whereas fear and doubt are mind based; you know because caution doesn't put you in a corner and make you quiver. It warns you in a beneficial yet unobtrusive way.

One of the obvious issues with chronic doubt and fear is that these forces originate from, feed off of, and breed heavy negativity. Considering that everything you say, do, think, and feel can color your intentions, actions, and belief system, you can see why this is a problem. Fear and doubt encourage you to begin each day with a poor sense of self and a discouraged outlook. When these themes permeate your life, your potential for happiness takes a nosedive because you're always waiting for the other shoe to drop. You may not fully invest in relationships because you don't expect them to last. You hide from new opportunities because you figure they're long shots or won't pay off anyway. As a result, you gravitate to safer and less-stimulating routes. Yet you probably also resent these choices and resent yourself for making them. At *best*, a humdrum path can lead to a predictable journey that you'll likely walk with regret, boredom, and a ton of misgivings. You may question who you are, how you got to this point, and how to stop the degrading cycle. To make matters worse, chronic doubt and fear can even cause you to doubt and fear your potential for happiness, so you might not even try to find it! You basically dump glue on an emotional and spiritual state that's already stuck in place. Good grief, no wonder you're blocked. Thankfully, your Team can guide you out of it.

Your angels and guides are adamant about dealing with situational and chronic doubt and fear because negative energy can block positive energy. When you are in the throes of doubt and fear, it's harder for your Team to intervene, for you to hear your instincts, and for you to believe in a stable and positive reality in your future. It also invites more negative energy into your immediate field, whether it belongs to ugly situations or peers who bring you down. Clients who struggle with doubt and fear tell me they repeatedly "find themselves" in negative situations and among toxic people, but when you make decisions from a point of fear or doubt, it's more likely that *you're putting yourself* in bad situations. You don't need me to tell you that misery loves company, so those with negative habits and a sour outlook will gravitate to you, and you to them, when doubt and fear play a big role in your life. You'll find solace in shared perspectives and feel comfortable around the lower energy you both give off.

When another person's doubt or fear becomes dangerous to you, your Team takes this very seriously. It reminds me of my client Sasha, who saw me for a reading after her mother passed. Her mom's soul stepped forward right away as part of Sasha's Team. Mom told me that Sasha fears she's a letdown to herself and her family because she's an alcoholic and uses drugs; she doubts she'll ever amount to much more than the person she is now. Mom then showed me that Sasha had been trying to take a trip but was continually thwarted. When I mentioned this, Sasha validated it—"I was trying to get concert tickets with friends in Chicago, but I'm not having any luck. I've tried three times now! Is Mom going to help?" Spirit laughed because they showed me that Sasha's angels and spirit guides had actually been blocking her trip. Their reasoning was that by going to the concert, she'd feel tempted to use and drink. "Don't put yourself in that position. You're too close to recovery," her Team asked me to tell Sasha. "Your instincts even told you this would be a bad idea." My guides then showed me a broom, which, if you remember, is my sign for when you need to sweep toxic people and situations out of your life. "Start listening to your intuition, and cut out the nonsense," I channeled from Mom.

In this chapter, you'll use Believe, Ask, and Act to disable the thoughts that feed doubt and fear so you can make confident, informed choices. Doubt and fear come from your mind, so they exist only when you fuel them with the anxiety and negative thinking they need to thrive.

Believe

- Believe that your soul is always united with God's energy, which ensures unending potential and unconditional love. You have no reason for alarm and nothing to question because you're safe, understood, and cared for by the universe. God has given you the tools to meet life's challenges—navigational instincts, a Universal Team, and the potential for self-awareness, control, love, and balance—and they're all accessible from within. With this comes the power to endure. Every day arrives with some risk and reward, but we all possess the strength to overcome doubt and fear. The light of God lives in each of us, and it drives the human spirit.

- Believe that when you devote ardent, consistent energy to worry, the universe responds to this as if it's a long-term meditation, and you will encourage negative energy that muddies your path. If instead you focus on solution-oriented thinking and believe that positive outcomes will be yours, that is what you will attract. Believe that God did not create doubt and fear and that these forces do not come from God, because God is unlimited love. Doubt and fear are learned emotions that are acquired through life experience. They simply exist on this plane, but if you let them overtake you, you'll veer off your best path. You'll overlook beauty and wonder because you're so focused on doubt and fear.

- Believe that while God honors prayers that arise because you feel doubt and fear, you shouldn't *only* turn to God when you are scared or uncertain. You also can't expect that because you look to God when you are afraid, He will reward you for coming to Him by answering all your prayers. Know that every prayer is heard by God and your Team, and He will sustain you when you feel doubt and fear.

- Believe that when you encounter doubt and fear, you will answer with faith. Faith that you and your Team can navigate any waters. Faith that you are strong enough to push past obstacles. Faith that you are here to thrive. Your faith should be bigger than your fears and concerns. Ask your Team to send signs that proffer hope. "Your guides and angels will always have a rope," my guides say. "If you can see even a pinpoint of light and can focus on that, hold on."

There's an old saying that goes "A ship in the harbor is safe, but that's not what ships are built for." I love that. No matter what storm you encounter, God wants you to press on without doubt and fear. My client David was a prosecuting attorney who dedicated his life to putting away criminals; he had a high-risk, high-reward job, but he couldn't wait to retire. Shortly after he left his law firm, his mom and sister died within a year of each other. Six months later, he had heart surgery and experienced a rare complication; the operation cut off bloodflow to his spinal cord and paralyzed him from the waist down. Yet despite all David has suffered and lost, he Believes in God's goodness and has no doubt or fear about what tomorrow holds. He's more likely to say "Thank you, God" than "Why me?" or "How will I go on?" David Believes life is meant to be lived, so he revels in telling stories to his grandchildren about his "good life." Spirit showed me that David never wavers in his faith, so doubt and fear are a nonissue. David's setbacks haven't taken precedence over all he has done and is as a person. He endures and learns from his experiences in a positive and inspiring way that buoys his soul and sustains his everyday life.

Your Turn

Affirm your belief that you can overcome doubt and fear by thinking or saying, "I Believe that with God and Spirit's guidance, I will have the confidence to achieve all that is intended for me with bravery and certainty."

Ask

Whether your fear is situational or chronic, Spirit wants you to Ask questions that guide you to the root of your concern so you can understand and address where it's coming from. For instance, imagine that you are considering taking a job but are worried that it doesn't align with your career path. Perhaps the reason for your doubt and fear is not really that you question the actual prospect, but is more because you worry about your ability to make sound choices for yourself on a larger scale. Perhaps your self-doubt stems from overprotective parents who discouraged you to think and act independently, and this influence bled into other areas of your life. Once you realize the sources of your doubt and fear, you're better poised to Act.

Understanding your doubt and fear and where they come from is an imperative step to growth since these complex emotions don't have a cookie-cutter presentation. They manifest based on how you feel in the situation at hand, so forward motion relies on your ability to honestly reflect with Spirit's help. In an unraveling relationship, for example, doubt and fear could cause you to either fight too hard *or* too little for what you want. Figuring out your motivating factors helps you clarify your intentions.

My client Josie struggles with chronic fear and anxiety; she'd give the Debbie Downer character from *Saturday Night Live* a run for her money. Josie's fear touches everything in her life, from her health to her family dynamics and self-image. If her two-year-old granddaughter pushes the dog, she's sure the child will become a bully some day. If a blood test shows she's anemic, Josie assumes it's cancer. If her husband has a disagreement with his boss, she's certain he'll be fired and they'll plummet into debt. She also changes jobs a lot because she thinks her peers are out to get her. And on it goes. The result? Josie's constant panic blocks her from joy. Because her sour outlook is exhausting, her friendships are short lived and her family limits visits. If Josie could decrease her doubt and fear, she'd be so much happier.

I encouraged Josie to use Believe, Ask, and Act to tame her hesitations, and she told me she found the Ask step especially enlightening. In meditation, she was shown multiple ways her own mom acted out of doubt and fear and that repeating her mother's patterns felt like "home." She also felt that perhaps her anxieties escalated after her mother passed away. Josie realized that just because she comes from a long line of matriarchal naysayers, her attitude doesn't make her happy, and she felt determined to break the legacy. Josie took her shot at redemption when, during a routine maintenance check, her mechanic found that her car's coolant was leaking. Ordinarily Josie would've thought, *Of course my car is a lemon. I'm destined to break down on a back road somewhere in the dark of night, and God knows what will happen to me then.* Instead, she stopped short of a deep sigh and thanked her angels and guides for alerting her to the engine issue before her car overheated and caused her serious and expensive damage.

Because doubt and fear are so disabling, Spirit says that angels and guides will work extra hard to help you feel reassured of their presence and safe in their care during Ask—but you do have to Ask for their assistance first. So when listening for answers, you may sense multiple responses—certainly during meditation or prayer, but also as outside advice and other signs. In fact, I strongly encourage you to turn to confidants for guidance because Spirit likes to work through them, too. This is like when my friend Caroline felt situational fear when her neighbor's moving man was staring at her in a scary, lewd way. She wasn't sure what to do; it wasn't enough of an offense to call the police, and she didn't want to confront and risk angering the man since he knew where she lived. The scenario made Caroline feel paralyzed, so she used Believe, Ask, and Act to resolve it. She Asked in prayer, "Am I in danger?" and heard that she should call a few friends for their input, all of whom said the same thing—he likely wouldn't harm her. She thanked Spirit for reassuring her through a consensus but also thought, *I still wish I had another option.* Within *seconds,* a friend unfamiliar with the situation coincidentally asked her out for coffee, and when Caroline told her about the strange guy, the woman insisted Caroline stay at her house until her husband was home from work. Caroline loved her Team's backup plan and felt at peace.

Your Turn

I'd like you to choose one situation that's causing you situational or chronic fear that you suspect may be blocking you. Perhaps you doubt that your girlfriend is serious about you (situational), or you're afraid that you alienate every new friend you meet (chronic). Anything more general—like "Why do I always feel afraid?"—is too vague a question to make any sizeable difference in your thoughts or actions, so be sure to pick a specific incident or situation that embodies your experience of doubt or fear.

Call on an angel, guide, or cultural figurehead that represents protection to you—think Native American warrior guides, powerful gladiators, and strong Egyptian goddesses. These are just some of the souls that step forward during doubt and fear discussions with clients. You can also Ask for a faith-based soul or angel of protection to help you address these questions, and when an image appears in your head, trust that your guides placed it there. While I was channeling this advice, Archangel Michael appeared with his arms stretched out to me and said, "Place your fear within my hands and know you are protected." He's a great one to call on!

The runway to this Ask step is longer than most because fear is impossible for Spirit to penetrate if it dominates your energy field. To settle into a relaxing headspace, let's move out of your mind and into your body. Start by taking three deep breaths in and out. As you breathe in, think *Inhale strength and protection* and while breathing out, *Exhale doubt and fear.* Next, notice how your body is reacting to your fearful thoughts and use motion to release the energy. So if your shoulders are raised and tense, shrug them a few times. If your neck is sore, move your head from side to side. Notice how the muscles and tendons loosen. Another option is to sit in Yogi pose and imagine yourself wrapped in a blanket of beautiful, golden energy. Imagine it flowing around and through your body. Do this until you feel a wave of peace, quiet, and calm settle over you. You may even feel the energy tingle from within your body a bit.

Once you feel relaxed and centered, envision yourself protected in a bubble of white light and imagine three cords quickly locking you into the ground. With the soul you chose in mind, state this intention: "I have the strength to overcome the doubt and fear that hold me back." Then calmly Ask your Team the "six Ws"—who, what, when, where, why, and how. When my guardian angel suggested this approach, I smiled at the idea of using the basic questions that police officers use during an investigation! Spirit clearly wants you to get to the bottom of your doubts and fears as efficiently as possible. You can do this meditation in one long, deep session or break it up as your schedule allows.

Sense Spirit's answers, stay open to guidance, and don't forget to thank your Team for their help.

Who

Who am I hurting the most with this doubt and fear?

What

What is the situation causing me doubt and fear?

What does it specifically make me feel?

What makes these feelings subside or escalate?

When

When did I first begin feeling this way?

When do I feel, or have I felt, relief or safety from these feelings?

Are there any commonalities here?

Where

Where can I go—mentally or physically—to feel reassurance and calm in the midst of panic?

Why

Why am I holding on to this doubt and fear?

How

How can I take my first step toward feeling confident, strong, and safe?

Act

With a better grip on your fear and doubt, you will be able to Act to eliminate their power, regain control, and use your instincts to move on. Act is a particularly challenging step when you're wrestling with doubt and fear, because the nature of these forces commits you to a standstill. I suggest you address Act in baby steps, since you'll make incremental changes you can see and there's less room to feel overwhelmed by the process. Pace yourself and assess how you feel after each step while following Spirit's direction.

This is exactly what my client Christine did, and it worked out beautifully. At nineteen years old, she designed a shapewear line; a few years later, she sold it to a large corporation. In her early twenties, the self-made millionaire got married and jumped into other seemingly lucrative ventures like real estate and tech, but these bubbles kept bursting before her eyes. By her midforties, Christine's marriage also ended, and she struggled to reinvent herself professionally. She was confused and had lost faith in her abilities and a higher power's "willingness" to help her out. Christine didn't understand why life wasn't flowing for her the way it once did. She was so afraid that her next venture would be another bust that she opted to do nothing. Christine was frozen in place, and every time she brainstormed new ideas, she felt overwhelmed, doubted her instincts, and questioned her abilities. This is when she came to see me.

With Spirit's guidance, Christine and I began to dissect her fears and doubts. She felt anxious that she'd been on a losing streak. Her divorce had taken a bite out of her self-esteem, which caused her to question her overall value to others. Before we could go on, Spirit suggested that Christine Ask her guides and angels one question: "What do I love to do?" Christine was shown that for the past twenty years, she'd successfully helped a lot of friends envision and launch their businesses, even when her own ideas hit a wall. And she had fun every time! "I might as well get paid for it!" she laughed, and planned to Act right away. In a few weeks' time, Christine launched a business to help entrepreneurs succeed.

Because Christine listened to her instincts, her Team provided her with incredible opportunities; and to avoid feeling swamped with responsibility, she Acted on each in baby steps. Wouldn't you know, the very first client Christine met was a lingerie designer? She smiled at the synchronicity, recognized the sign, and thanked her angels and guides for the gift. What's interesting is that this designer didn't just ask for Christine's help as a consultant; he asked her to partner with him in his business. This put Christine back in her element—with not one, but now two businesses to run, so over the next few months, she paced herself. A little at a time, she met new contacts, vendors, and partners, pausing to weigh the pros and cons with each. Her past businesses taught her that the market could change on a dime, so thoughtful motion was a must. Though Christine's steps were gradual, purpose returned to her life almost immediately. And at a work appointment, Christine bumped into an old high school crush; after some time, the two began dating and eventually got married. If all that's not enough, when I last saw Christine, she told me that her lingerie partner introduced her to an accessories designer who may help expand their line even further! Since Christine employed her Team's baby steps, her life has completely turned around.

You'll know you're Acting without doubt and fear when you feel confident about your future. This does not mean that you won't still have questions about what the right next step is or that you won't do frequent self-checks to ensure that your decisions feel like the best ones you can make. But rather than being crippled by indecision, you will feel like you are taking sensible steps to gather information and really weigh your options. You may turn to others for input, but you won't need them to validate every decision you make. You won't be as hard on yourself about your choices because you'll know that whatever you do next, Spirit's steered you there for a reason, if just to inform your next move. You'll enjoy yourself and feel calm in new situations, perform your best, and not feel self-conscious. Acting with confidence isn't so much about holding yourself in high esteem as it is about accepting who you are so you can enjoy what you're doing. When you demonstrate self-worth, you believe in an intrinsic competence that comes from your soul.

Your Turn

Your Act steps will be determined by what you sensed during Ask, but when you're ready to make your first tangible move that commits you to forward motion, Spirit offers a tip. If your goal is to call the lawyer, send your boss an e-mail, or make the doctor's appointment, start by listing three things that will help you make each daunting move. Maybe you can write down what you want to say to the lawyer, rehearse it with a friend, and edit your final thoughts before you pick up the phone. Put a check next to each achievement because this will make you feel accomplished; it will feed positivity and motivate you to keep going. If you take to this process, you can use the technique during the rest of your Act steps, too.

CHAPTER 9

Break Down the Great Wall of Grief

There's a big difference between missing a loved one and being weighed down by grief. And when a person you love passes away, it's hard to make sense of your feelings and carry on in their absence. I've suffered much loss in my life, plus I've channeled a lot of clients' loved ones and have come to believe that death is just a moment—like ripping off a bandage—that transitions us from this life to the next leg of our soul's path. It's painful and difficult that those of us left behind battle worldly feelings like grief, but Spirit explains that while you never "get over" your sorrow, you must not let it overcome you. Your Team asks that you navigate through it, learn to coexist with it, and carry on with your journey in this world.

Like so many of my clients, I've questioned why sudden deaths and tragedies occur, and my guides' answers are very matter-of-fact: "Without death, your journey here can't end and continue on." Accidents, tragedies, and loss are part and parcel for how the soul progresses; and the universe doesn't intend for these to stop *your* life in its tracks. And while the emotional gravity of death is greater than that of most obstacles, coexisting with grief is simply another challenge that we must navigate on this plane. Spirit wants you to lean on your Team to help you get up each morning, be there for the living who love and need you, and try your best to gradually heal. Healing is not forgetting but accepting how to live with your grief, carry on with your life, and continue to honor and love those who've passed.

Holding on to grief will keep you from happiness in so many ways, and it is a tremendous block from both worldly and energetic perspectives; the symbol I'm shown when a client is struggling with overwhelming grief is actually a brick wall. Like living in the past or remaining in your comfort zone, grief causes your life and energy to become stuck in place. Clutching to such a heavy, distracting, and negative emotion can hinder relationships, create anger, impair your faith, cause you to feel hopeless, tempt you to isolate yourself, and make you feel generally unloved and alone. It also keeps you from being present for those who need you, because you're so focused on the past or a person who's no longer here. It becomes harder to listen to your own instincts when you're consumed by sorrow.

What I've often seen happen is that the heavy energy of grief actually blocks departed loved ones, and therefore they can't reach out with support and guidance that might make the pain of loss more bearable. They can't nudge your instincts or help you feel their presence. They can't direct your attention to signs (you might also miss their signs if you're too sad to notice them). Spirit merges their energy with yours to create visits in dreams, but they can't do this when your energy is too low for the union—and if they do find a way to push through, your sadness usually skews the dream's interpretation anyway.

My client Jess was deeply grieving the sudden death of her husband, Lyle. He passed in a car accident because he wasn't wearing a seat belt despite the countless times Jess warned him about this. Because Jess was angry about Lyle's passing, she often dreamed about Lyle leaving her—and in one dream, her husband's actual soul appeared. Jess was thrilled at first because she could tell by how "real" the encounter felt that it was truly his soul. Lyle stood still, smiling, and then disappeared. Short and sweet, as visits in dreams often are. Sadly, Jess didn't interpret his brevity this way; she woke up convinced that Lyle was mad at her because he left the dream so abruptly. During a reading, Lyle told me he'd appeared to comfort Jess, but her heavy energy controlled the dream's tone. To fix this misunderstanding, I suggested Jess stop replaying Lyle's death in her mind and focus on a happy memory right before bed. This raised her vibration. In a few weeks' time, Lyle tried again, and Jess welcomed the love she felt from his soul during her dream state; it really helped her heal.

In addition to showing me a brick wall, Spirit makes me experience heaviness and grief exactly as the person is feeling it at that time. When it's crippling, they insist you find ways to compartmentalize so this sorrow doesn't take over your life. Ask your Team for support because they want to help. While there's a thin veil between you and your loved ones, they can see your life in vignettes. They *are* still with you, more actively than you might ever imagine. When you accept your grief, the universe allows their souls to engage in worldly moments that show you they're near. Acceptance is both emotionally beneficial and practical since it opens you up to your loved ones' comfort.

I'm shown that, second only to doubt and fear, a grief block can create the most negative ripple effect a person feels on this plane. There are many known stages of grief—including denial, anger, bargaining, and acceptance—and there are layers of sadness, depression, confusion, pain, and loneliness within each. This is why sitting with a medium after a loved one dies can have a profound effect. In my experience, it addresses so many of these complicated feelings via direct answers from a soul and streamlines the path to acceptance that they're safe, at peace, and still part of our lives. That said, no matter how personal the information in a reading is, Spirit's overwhelming message is always the same: Respect your grief and honor your loved ones, but don't let grief cause the rest of your life to spin out of control. Do your best to keep going without them.

Though a lot of blocks are related to your choices, I want to be clear that Spirit isn't saying you're defiantly choosing to feel blue—as if your sadness is selfish, lazy, or unwarranted, because none of those things is true. Of course you'd rather feel motivated to go out or laugh more easily than you do when you're in the thick of sadness. But sometimes, Spirit says you may cling to grief because you're afraid to let go; staying in that sorrow might make a loved one's memory feel more present. You might feel it's disrespectful or disloyal to stop grieving or somehow insensitive to do an activity that makes you feel good, especially if the person died tragically.

You might even be concerned about how people will perceive the way you're grieving and get sucked into a downward spiral in an effort to show outwardly how much you've been impacted by a loss. Maybe you have guilt or regrets, felt that words were left unspoken, had a challenging relationship, or didn't get to say goodbye. These situations can further lower your energy and thicken the wall. And so you hold on to the emptiness because it feels warranted and real. But if your life's falling apart and sadness is swallowing your identity, your soul's path will veer out of your control. Perhaps today you don't care or feel ready to continue on your journey, but at some point you will need to pick up the pieces. Isn't it better to do this before grief's ripple effect can do any more damage?

Processing loss is a daily practice, and how a person grieves and how long it takes until they heal are very personal. There is no right way, and there isn't one acceptable time window. I'm not a grief counselor, but in this chapter, I will share the beliefs that Spirit says will start and in some cases further the healing process. These practices can also release the energy that's blocking your ability to connect with loved ones and move toward acceptance. I'll suggest ways to feel your Team's support, guidance, and protection as your brick wall comes down and how to maintain a relationship with your passed loved ones that is both healthy and fruitful.

Believe

- Believe that your loved ones are safe and at peace and have a productive existence in Heaven. They're happy and thriving on the Other Side and still very much connected to you. Your faith plays a large role in releasing a grief block because beliefs about the Other Side can help you accept a loved one's passing, which allows loved ones to reach you and for you to embrace life without them. "Know that we are near you, and that life goes on after you leave this plane," my father-in-law's soul tells me. "Know you can feel a connection to the Other Side and to us because there is a thin veil between you and the souls in Heaven." He says it's almost as if your loved ones are in the next room; they're that close. That makes me feel so comforted and reassures me that we remain connected.

- Believe that departed loved ones are with you when you need them—during good and bad experiences—because your love is a bond and connection that will never be broken. A fun bit of proof is that Spirit loves to attend meaningful celebrations. I've seen deceased family and friends show me that they put on a tux or fancy dress to attend a wedding or graduation in our world. And when you're blocked by grief, it's your loved ones who comfort you. Higher energies like angels and guides are all about your spiritual path, soul, purpose, and belief system; but more worldly energies, like humans who've crossed over, help you tread through relatable grievances when they sense you need them. During a reading, I might see a soul hold or pat your hand or rub your back. When spouses die, they show me an impression on your bed to tell you they still lie next to you at night. Children's souls climb all over parents' laps. Love bonds your soul to those of family and friends for eternity.

- Believe that on the Other Side, a soul's existence goes on. Just as your life has a purpose, the departed soul has moved on to continue its purpose in Heaven. When you die, you help better the universe from the Other Side, and your soul's path continues to evolve. If you want to pursue certain studies, skills, or interests for enjoyment's sake or to bring into your next life, you can. My favorite story about grief and belief, though, is about a girl named Kelly who died in an accident at twenty years old. During a reading with her mom shortly after Kelly passed, she showed me that, as a soul, she'd continue to intellectually progress on the Other Side—working to promote justice in some capacity—and that she'd meet and mother the children she'd raise in her next life, before they incarnate together. This was the first time I'd heard of a soul doing this, and Kelly's mother thought it was so wonderful since her daughter's early death precluded her from being a professional or mom in our world, which were Kelly's dreams.

     The news that Kelly's life would continue rocked her mom's

belief system in an incredible way. Because Kelly passed in the prime of her life, her mom was devastated to think her daughter would miss out on important milestones like developing a skill that makes an impact on our world or raising children. To know that Kelly's essence didn't end but instead went on to include these meaningful markers of adulthood made her mother's heart swell. It also expanded my client's religious belief that there's an afterlife with God in Heaven to include the specific nature of Kelly's path and sources of happiness.

- Believe that your own soul needs you to heal. This allows you to create balance in your life again so you're able to understand that, even without a loved one, life continues for both of you. You are not meant to experience constant pain, sorrow, regret, or heartache. Healing helps your soul refocus and move back onto the path you are meant to be on. By facing your grief and refusing to let it overcome you, you raise your vibration back to where it needs to be so you can allow for happiness and positive emotion to flow into your life again. Grief no longer becomes a roadblock but yet another experience that informs your character and imprint.

- Believe that as you move on in a positive way, so do your loved ones. When clients tell me they could once feel their loved ones around them after they passed but not as much in recent weeks or months, the soul often says it's because they've grown and ascended to another spiritual plane. I even had one soul say, "You might not understand where I am, but I always make my way back to you."

- Believe in what you're meant to know about the Other Side but also in the mystery of God's larger plan. Understand that the great unknown is exactly that—great—and when you get to the Other Side, your questions will be answered and replaced with new questions. You'll proceed to other and higher realms of consciousness and continue to add to your imprint. If you knew everything about the afterlife while on earth, you'd feel halfway to Heaven. But you are worldly and have to trust the process of how your worldly soul completes its life cycle, knowing that it's preparation for what's to come.

Your Turn

Affirm your belief that you can coexist with your grief by thinking or saying, "I Believe God has a plan, and with each day that I have faith, I will focus less on my grief and more on my own journey."

Ask

Spirit says that seeing, feeling, and receiving signs from loved ones can help lift a grief block because it takes the sting out of "living without them." The tangible signs let you know that their souls are, in fact, with you. So for this Ask, let's focus on requesting, recognizing, and receiving signs. Up to this point, Spirit's asked you to look for signs that can be used as tangible stepping-stones that lead to a focused goal. When Asking for a loved one's signs here, they, too, can be seen as stepping-stones but toward an emotional conviction to accept your grief and know that your loved ones' souls are a big part of your life.

Do not give Spirit parameters about what the sign should be or when or how often you should receive it (as in "Send me a license plate message by tomorrow!"). Your Team appreciates specificity in prayer requests, but don't put restrictions on loved ones here because different energies have different capabilities. They also use what's available at the moment; it's unfair to ask for live butterflies in the middle of winter and then expect Spirit to deliver! When you Ask for signs, trust they will come. Spirit's signs might not arrive right away, yet they will show up soon enough. And again, the faster you put grief in its place, the more signs you'll get and the greater your awareness and guidance will be. The more you Believe in signs, the more they will happen because you're opening up. You'll also hear, feel, and see more from all the souls on your Team because you're exercising your instincts to do this.

Spirit uses its energy to direct your attention toward the symbol so that you'll notice it. When it comes to signs, Spirit likes to stick with those you've heard of, too. It's a little like branding; they want you to recognize what is around you. Spotting signs can be emotionally challenging enough that Spirit doesn't want to make it any harder to find them. Pennies, dragonflies, feathers, birds, numerical sequences, and song lyrics are a few common signs Spirit uses because they've become culturally recognizable.

So how *do* you spot a sign from a loved one? One of two events must occur. Either you will look at the sign, and the person who passed will pop into your head at that time or immediately after; or you will think about the person, and moments later you'll receive the sign—sometimes it will arrive on its own and sometimes you will need to Ask for it. This last point reminds me of how my client Cyndi had been missing her pop when she Asked, "Pop, please send me a sign." She then hopped in the car on her way to the mall to go shopping, flipped on the radio, and Beyoncé's "Halo" was playing. She had an immediate sense of knowing that this was her pop's doing, as halos reminded her of Heaven and she'd turned it on at the start of the refrain.

Loved ones can use their energy in very clever ways when sending signs. They can focus it to pull your attention in a certain direction, create serendipitous opportunities, or give you an overall feeling of peace. They can use their energy to touch your head or shoulder or create the feeling that someone is standing next to you. Because Spirit can channel through your mind, they can also make suggestions and set up clever interactions knowing what's ahead. It reminds me of how my client Jeffrey swore he hadn't received a sign from his father in twenty years, yet when I channeled his dad's soul, he began throwing coins around the room in my mind's eye. He said he'd been trying to penetrate his son's grief all along, although Jeffrey hadn't been able to see it because he was so overwhelmed with his pain. When I asked Jeffrey what the coins meant, he explained that for the past week, he'd paid for everything in coins—to the point that it had become a family joke. Here, the father's energy prompted Jeffrey to use mostly change, knowing he'd mention it in the reading. Coins then became the sign his father said he'd send from then on.

You don't need a reading to establish a sign with your loved one, though. You can do it before a person passes or state it aloud or in your mind anytime after they die. The soul will honor both. If you begin to notice how your loved ones' souls interact with you and what it feels like when they do, you can try to make sure you don't miss an encounter. Don't become obsessed with noticing signs, but if something happens that seems a little odd, try to make sense of it.

My client Isabelle and her husband, Paul, were on vacation when Paul said out of the blue that the neighborhood they were driving through reminded him of the area where her cousin Maryellen, who'd died a few years earlier, once lived. The area looked *nothing* like that to Isabelle, and though they hadn't talked about Maryellen in a while, Isabelle had been missing her a lot in the past few days. This made Isabelle suspect that Paul's random comment might be prompted by Spirit, based on how she'd been feeling. Isabelle casually sent a text message to Maryellen's son Donnie to say hi, and as "coincidence" would have it, he was in the same vacation town for a wedding that weekend. Isabelle sensed they should all meet for drinks, and Donnie said he was actually on his way to a bar for a private party but didn't indicate which one. As Isabelle received this text, Paul parked in the only spot available, which, as it turned out, was right in front of Donnie's bar. Isabelle knew without a doubt that her cousin's soul arranged this catch-up session and was with them the whole time, particularly since Maryellen asked Isabelle to stay in touch with her son after she passed.

Realize that Spirit's signs will change as you have different needs and the soul's energy evolves. My friend Collin, for instance, used to always notice a blue jay that he felt was being sent from his departed uncle; then one day, he stopped seeing it. A few weeks later, Collin began to really feel his uncle's presence when his friends began using phrases and clichés his uncle once used during their own conversations. As he gradually healed, Collin no longer craved visual cues and could appreciate more verbal messages. A soul's abilities change as the soul evolves, too. Perhaps its energy could only offer feelings of comfort shortly after it passed, but now it can flicker lights or direct your attention to a clock at symbolic times of the day.

The more you Ask for and recognize Spirit's reassurance, the more your grief wall will crumble. You'll feel at peace, and sorrow won't consume your every thought. A faint sadness may always be a hand on your shoulder, but you'll be able to focus on a more positive or productive thought about what's going on in your day.

Some of my all-time favorite signs have come from my father-in-law, James, in an effort to get his wife's attention. For instance, my kids were dancing to a One Direction video on TV in the bedroom that my mother-in-law shared with James, and it was so silly that she filmed it on her iPhone. Later, when she played it back after we'd all left, she called me *screaming*. On the footage, you can actually see a bright blue orb about the size of an orange take shape and then move on a clear, direct path around the kids and then toward the door, which is where my mother-in-law was standing! I'll also never forget when she wanted to honor James's memory by continuing an annual tradition of going into Manhattan on their anniversary. The problem was, she'd always relied on James to lead her around, and now he couldn't. This made her really upset. Then one night, he came to her in a dream and said, "Look in the book." She had no idea what this meant, but the next day, she walked past a bag of his things sitting near the door and sensed, "Look in the bag." Sure enough, inside the bag was a book about golf that I'd given James, and tucked inside was a map of Manhattan!

Your Turn

I'd like you to make a series of requests to a deceased loved one you'd like to connect with, particularly if you sense this grief blocks you from carrying on. You'll present these as statements rather than questions, so listening for answers may feel different from in prior chapters. You may still hear or feel reassurance while you're sitting quietly, but most signs and opportunities will come after you've opened your eyes.

Among my clients, I've noticed that an inability to recognize signs is a little like my inability to recognize how carbs sabotage my diet. I don't seem to notice all the bread and pretzels I eat until I consciously bring my attention to the subject and become aware of each bite that enters my mouth. Food diaries help with this! In that vein, I'd like you to keep a written tally of how many times you receive a sign to see how often loved ones are with you, feel grateful for that, and help you open up even more.

When you're ready to begin, take a moment to quiet, ground, and protect yourself. Ask your deceased loved one by name to please come forward. State the intention: "I open my eyes, mind, and soul to trust and receive your signs." Then place the requests below. For a month, I'd like you to jot down signs like the song whose lyrics felt meaningful, the cardinal that appeared in the window when you were thinking of your deceased father, or the feather that landed in your lap while you were reminiscing about your late aunt. At the end of each week, read what you've written and marvel at how the universe blesses those who pay attention. Stay open to and aware of Spirit's presence, and express gratitude for their guidance.

Requests to Sense a Loved One

Please send me a sign or let me feel you near me. Show me you're around.

Please visit me in meditation or a dream.

Please show me my next steps to help me coexist with my grief.

Act

You will never stop missing your loved ones, but their souls always insist that you find a way to live with your grief and carry on without them. Act, then, is about compartmentalizing sadness—setting time aside to honor your loved ones and putting those feelings in a safe place so you can turn back to the living.

Spirit's favorite exercise for grief blocks is telling clients to picture all your priorities and concerns filed in a private cabinet—finances, relationships, work, and so on. Then mentally add to this a folder labeled "Grief" that's separate from other areas of your life. Pull out the folder when you can spend time feeling your feelings—alone at the beach, at a support group, with a friend. Have a good cry and be in that moment. This will help you live with grief rather than suppress or allow it to subsume you.

As you Act, be sure to lean on friends and family who want to help, and allow them to support you however you need. Our souls are energetic sponges, and there's no better time to absorb other people's good intentions than when you're suffering and unable to summon this on your own. Help can come from therapists, friends, church members, support groups. Grief is an emotional state that can feel very isolating, so let other people in. It's too hard to work through the healing process alone. "Expression and companionship are important to the soul, so do not rob your healing process of this," my guides say.

Though it may help to put grief in its proverbial box, keep the lid to conversation open with loved ones' souls. Chats can happen formally, like at a graveyard or church, or you can talk with them while pulling weeds, straightening your hair, or making breakfast. Complain about your busy weekend, tell them how nervous you are about a job interview, and share how much they're missed. I had a client who woke up every morning and said, "Good morning, Mom!" after her mother passed; I know this because when I channeled Mom's soul, the first thing she said was "Good morning, honey!" Talk to your loved ones as if they were in the same room—their energy is all around you! You can also speak to them in your mind. In this vein, writing to them can be a cathartic activity. Spirit can hear any thoughts specifically directed at them.

For most of my clients, I know their wall of grief is crumbling when they actually want to spend more time with the living. My client Krissy was very close to her grandma Elle while she was alive, and every year, she gathered family to honor and celebrate Elle's memory at a family picnic. This almost posed a problem for Krissy when one year her best friend got married on the same date as the gathering. Though Krissy hesitated to let go of Grandma's big day, she was happy to attend her friend's wedding instead. She knew it was time to move on, and she couldn't think of a better person to spend the day with.

As you Act, you'll find that your Team will open your eyes to your life as it exists now, without your loved one. When you cling to grief, you very much cling to the past—memories, regrets, what-ifs, and what you wish would/could/should have happened. Spirit wants you to accept how your life has changed and Act in your current reality as best you can.

When my client Jamie lost her husband, Alex, to a heart attack, she dropped out. She rarely saw friends, stopped seeing her nieces whom she's close to, and adopted a dog to keep her company. She exhausted herself thinking about how despondent Alex's death made her, how they'd never have a family together, and how their life might have played out if he'd lived. This went on for years, as Jamie noticed that friends called less often, her nieces made memories without her, and her dog offered more isolation than comfort. During a reading, Alex pointed out that while Jamie never imagined a life without him, her current stagnancy wasn't a life she ever wanted either. After leaving me, Jamie used Believe, Ask, and Act to figure out how to compartmentalize the situation and embrace her new reality.

When it was time to Act, Jamie sensed that if she'd take just one positive step to move past the residual effects of grief, she'd feel emboldened to take another, then another. She Asked Alex to show her what to do first and felt that tidying up her space would breathe new life into it. "Unclutter your home, unclutter your mind," my guides like to say. So she organized her closet and shampooed her dog-hair-laden rugs. With her house now clean, Jamie felt motivated to cook instead of order takeout, so she began grocery shopping. As she established more control over what she ate, Jamie realized how unhealthy she'd become, so she joined a gym. Not only did Jamie lose ten pounds, but she met a new group of friends, and she still sees them for a treadmill endorphin rush whenever she's feeling down. Just as Jamie sensed, a positive domino effect took place during Act. She's more confident now because she no longer sees herself as the tragic widow figure she was but as the person she's become. Jamie misses Alex every day, but instead of remaining stuck in her grief, and thus stuck in her life, she goes on. She talks to his soul all the time, and she believes he can see how far she's come and that he's proud of her. I know he is, too. Jamie's found the balance between honoring Alex's memory and being present for herself.

Your Turn

Even as you heal, Spirit wants you to continue honoring your departed loved ones because your soul is eternally bonded to theirs. To do this, create three moments during the month where you and your loved one can spend time together. Maybe you can visualize a conversation with that soul, make their favorite meal, and connect with a mutual friend. In doing so, you fold them into your life as it exists now rather than revolving your life around a negative and heavy feeling from the past. Thinking about our loved ones or doing something nice in their honor also creates an immediate connection to their soul on the Other Side.

CHAPTER 10

Help Your Body Help You

Your body is the vehicle your soul uses to get through life, so you must keep it in good health. This means listening to your doctor, pursuing preventive measures so your body performs at its best, and learning what makes you feel good living in it. Your connection to the universe also depends on a healthy body, as it's one aspect of mind, body, and soul balance. Your head needs to stay sharp, your feelings intact, and your body in good shape so your entire being functions as optimally as it can in this realm. "It's your responsibility to take care of your body," my guides say. "It's a gift. You should treat it as one."

Though I'm going to focus primarily on your physical body in this chapter, Spirit says a person's entirety is more than just one body. In addition to your physical body, you also have mental (including emotional) and spiritual bodies. Each body can disrupt your life if it's out of whack, but concerns with the physical body cause my clients the most obvious struggle; those are the issues they can feel and describe in a palpable way that can limit their lifestyles. And while all bodies benefit each other, your physical body is the backbone of your existence on this plane. It aids with literal forward motion and can protect your other bodies from harm. Putting nourishing food into your body and moving it often can improve your mood and sharpen your mind. Decreasing the stress your body feels makes you less vulnerable to conditions like cancer, heart disease, and diabetes. And when your soul lives in a strong body, practices like meditation, which also boost your health, work from an optimal baseline.

Spirit says that physical health conditions arise when your mind, body, and soul are out of balance. To my understanding, your body's health, and health in general, is part of a nonspecific and rather subjective mind, body, soul equation that insists you use every modality you believe in to support it. The way you can best assess if you're maintaining your overall health is if you feel good in all three categories. If, however, you're depressed or suffering from a recent lack of faith, for example, this primes the body for a physical ailment to take hold, and you can't fully recover without putting all three bodies back into harmony. The same goes for a physical issue; all the medicine in the world won't fully eradicate the condition's impact if you carry negative feelings or behave in a way that isn't true to your imprint. The damage could affect you in a chronic, cellular, or energetic way because pain, suffering, and negative feelings over a health issue are sizeable impediments if they're not adequately addressed or navigated.

When Spirit wants me to address a client's health, the symbol I am shown is blood being drawn from an arm; and what I see or am told is usually a confirmation of what the client already knows. I don't see major illness or death. If your Team mentions a physical issue, then they're either validating that the steps you're taking are correct, suggesting a new direction, or telling you to get moving if you've done nothing at all. They might also prompt me to suggest integrative therapies like acupuncture, diet changes, or practices like yoga that can only help. To demonstrate that your Team knows what's going on, Spirit might ask me to scan your body for illness with my third eye and stop me when I reach the affected area to fill me in on what's going on. I once had a friend's Team take me on a "guided tour" inside her brain to explain what an MRI scan showed. This helped her understand the mechanics of her doctor's diagnosis.

If I *am* told your next step, this most often occurs with banal health concerns. So if you need to make a dentist appointment or go for a routine mammogram but still haven't checked it off your to-do list, your Team will remind you about it through me. Or maybe you're thinking about changing doctors or deliberating between two; your Team will offer guidance—maybe volunteer what they like about each one—but they won't make the choice for you. Once in a rare while, they'll dance around a diagnosis but in a covert way so neither I nor the client is startled. I'll never forget the time I picked up on my friend Shannon's heavy fatigue and said "something is going on with your thyroid." My guides didn't show me an outright mass, but Shannon did in fact have one when she followed up with her doctor the next week.

To get you to see a doctor, my Team tells me that yours might exaggerate symptoms, causing your imagination to run wild, or encourage you to seek testing or treatment for one illness that ultimately reveals a more pressing, "incidental" finding. My client Martin, after a random coughing episode, lost his balance and fell down the stairs on his way to grab cough drops. Worried about a concussion, his doctor ordered an MRI that showed a brain tumor unrelated to the fall. After surgery and a year of physical therapy, he's made a full recovery. Martin's Team definitely had a hand in his diagnosis and healing.

If you miss or don't pay attention to any abnormal symptoms you feel, your condition will obviously intensify on its own. But Spirit might also create roadblocks that oblige you to focus on your health. I've seen Teams slow down or halt a career, stall attempts at building a family, or prolong the selling of a house so the client is forced to pay attention to a health issue that needed their energy and commitment first. My client Esther, for example, is a manicurist who lost two jobs in a row due to unexpected layoffs. This was unusual for Esther, as she worked for private salons that courted *her* based on her loyal clientele and workaholic reputation. Shortly after losing her second job, however, Esther was diagnosed with breast cancer. When I heard this, I sensed that Spirit allowed her to be cut from both staffs so that she could devote as much time as she could to researching her disease and feeling good about her treatment. After a double mastectomy, Esther went into remission and knew it was time to return to work. But when she reflected on what she'd experienced, she decided it was time for a fresh start and opened her own salon. Having released her roadblock, she emerged a stronger, braver, and healthier version of herself and her business is booming.

To release a health block, your Team will place stepping-stones in your midst and try to make them as clear as possible. Sometimes the path is very straightforward, as when you find a doctor who immediately hands you an accurate diagnosis and treatment that works. Other times, they might take you on a more indirect route that isn't immediately obvious. I know what you're thinking: *Why doesn't Spirit just guide me to who will heal me as quickly as possible? Why would they allow it to become a game of Chutes and Ladders?* This is one of those answers that may only become clear in retrospect. Your path can be determined by various factors—urgency, a health issue's complexity, your ability to trust a first diagnosis, and maybe even lessons your soul is meant to learn. Your Team might also steer you to try other types of treatment methods (traditional and alternative), and it could take trial and error to find the best for you. Perhaps you'll meet new friends in waiting rooms or through doctors who become part of your support system. Healing your body is often like unpeeling an onion, and I've noticed that Spirit has a very "first things first" approach to achieving good health. What may feel like circuitous guidance may actually be Spirit prioritizing. They know that becoming well—whether you're trying to get in shape or heal a chronic condition—is a multilayered effort. It's like how my friend June decided she'd improve her health by running a marathon, yet felt frustrated when Spirit kept placing nutritionists in her path instead of trainers. To run her best time, however, Spirit knew June had to improve her eating habits and lose weight first; once she did that, she met a great trainer.

Know that you don't need to be fully healed for Spirit to release this block, since a health goal might take a while to reach or a more serious diagnosis could require long-term care. You simply need to acknowledge your concern, become determined to address it, and start following your Team's guidance. Also use this time to pray for healing and divine intervention. One of the wildest health experiences I've had was when Spirit stepped in while I was on the acupuncturist's table. I felt very imbalanced at the time; I was stressed over juggling family and work obligations, and I wasn't taking care of my body. As a result, my readings weren't as sharp as I'd like (when I don't take care of myself, my Team pulls the reins on my abilities; it's the first thing they block to get my attention). After the practitioner put her needles in me and closed the door, I looked up at the ceiling and my eyes went into a haze. I watched a green light trickle down all over my body like rain; I associate green light with the healing energy of Archangel Raphael, and this was a soothing reassurance that acupuncture was the right care for me at that time.

God has a remarkable plan for your body, too. In this chapter, I'll explore how your Team affects a healing journey, how to customize the guidance you need, and how to bring optimal health to fruition.

Believe

- Believe that you must treat your body as a temple even if it feels like a crumbling Greek ruin. I asked my guides why some of us were given bodies that malfunction and make us unhappy when we're meant to live a happy and full life. "The mechanisms of everyone's bodies are perfectly suited for your life span but also for the energy in your world," they told me. "The type of body you have is what helps you survive on the earth's level and plane. The human body is perfect in its imperfection and continues to evolve."

- Believe that having faith in God and your Team doesn't mean you'll never feel illness-related confusion, pain, or suffering. (You wouldn't believe how often I've heard, "I'm faithful to God and my church, so why am I so sick?") It means that as you strive to make your body stronger, God and your Team will guide, heal, and remain by your side. Don't wait until you're sick to turn to God and Spirit, though. You shouldn't suddenly start praying simply to get what you want or control what you'd like God to do for you.

Instead, you're meant to pray to put yourself in God's healing and unconditionally loving care.

- Believe that contrary to what some spiritual circles say, my guides say that negative emotions *can feed* sickness or a genetic predisposition, but they *cannot attract* sickness or be the sole cause of it. It is not that simple. So, for example, an inability to speak your mind won't attract or cause a sore throat. But if your body encounters a virus, it may be harder for your immune system to fight it if you're having communication issues, since the throat is the communication center of your body. Negative emotions can also fuel unhealthy habits, like drinking alcohol to numb emotional pain and developing liver issues as a result. Here, the sadness itself doesn't cosmically draw in a health issue, but your inclination to mask sadness with such an excess of alcohol does create a bona fide condition. Finally, you can't manifest diseases like cancer by being obsessively afraid of them. What will happen is that your fear will become so debilitating that it depletes your immune system, raises stress hormones, and keeps you from taking action to maintain or improve your health.

- Believe, on the other hand, that you can encourage healing by feeling and demonstrating positive emotions. Laughter, awe, gratitude, resilience, reconciliation, and socializing with positive people help alleviate the physical and energetic stress of negative feelings. After my client Marisa suffered a stroke, her husband asked family and friends to send as many cards as they could to show their encouragement. He hung them in the dining room until every surface was covered and bursting with visual proof of how much Marisa's family and friends loved her. While the cards didn't reverse the effects her stroke had on her body, they did make Marisa feel happy, appreciated, and supported with more good days than bad. They raised her vibration, which encouraged her to pursue treatments with optimism and hope. She allowed that positivity to motivate her through recovery as she worked to regain her strength and compensate for mild physical setbacks.

- Believe that the pursuit of good health is ongoing and that with each guided step, you're where you're meant to be at that moment. If you hit a wall or go as far as you can with one practitioner and need guidance toward finding a new one, that may even be part of Spirit's plan. I remember when my friend Liz, who has sciatica, saw an osteopath who modestly helped her. After a year, she moved on to another. Right away, she found her second doctor to be much more effective. This was great news for Liz's body. Rather than getting upset with Spirit for initially guiding her to a lesser doctor, she sensed that her Team's "misdirection" wasn't an accident. Liz realized that her first osteopath had a gentler bedside manner and simpler way of explaining the modality, and he came via a referral she trusted—all details Liz needed to help her Believe in the practice and Spirit's guidance. In other words, Liz's Team showed her the best option for her at the time; as soon as Liz acknowledged this, she felt immense faith and gratitude for her process.

- Believe that while the origin of sickness is physical, healing involves a spiritual leap of faith. Trust that God created you and knows your body's intricate inner workings. God can help heal what He made. And should your health really bring you down, Believe that God can do the impossible. No matter what your struggles, God will help you emerge with hope, courage, and certainty to move forward.

Your Turn

Affirm your belief that you can achieve optimal health by thinking or saying "I Believe in God's healing light. Let it guide and course through me from head to toe, helping to resolve what ails me."

Ask

As you Ask for guidance and healing, increase your awareness of your Team's stepping-stones. Try to pay more attention to coincidences, repetition, and fleeting hunches that point you in a specific direction, and follow them to their necessary ends. Of all the blocks we've discussed so far, health stepping-stones tend to be the most linear and literal. Rest assured your Team will be as specific and strategic as they can.

When your Team responds to your requests for health guidance, they're pretty direct about how they prompt next steps through your instincts. They don't mess around with clever signs and symbols unless it's to reassure you that your prayers are being heard. For instance, if you seek multiple opinions on a diagnosis, one will instinctually resonate while the others won't. Spirit also likes using your worldly resources to guide you, so you might find that you keep hearing about related stories or certain practitioners, which is Spirit's way of prompting you to look into them. I also love when Spirit uses its energy to draw your eye to an article or search result on Google; this is similar to how your loved ones use their energy to direct your attention to a bird or penny to say "hello" when you're thinking of them.

Your Team is a pro at finagling time-related issues, as well. Guides often show me how they help clients get into the doctor they're meant to see, create convenient schedules, and pace out multiple appointments in a way that allows them to inform each other. And if you're on the wrong course, Spirit may even create obstacles to get you back on path, especially if the direction has dire consequences. My client Lynn was experiencing a strange smattering of symptoms—fatigue, muscle aches, fevers, and spinal pain among them. She prayed for direction on how to navigate these issues, because they seemed to affect multiple body systems at once. Though Lynn's spinal pain was excruciating, she had a persistent hunch that she could have Lyme disease and got in to see a Lyme disease specialist before an orthopedist. Sure enough, her Lyme tests were positive. Her specialist immediately warned her that she should not receive steroid injections for her back because they could cause permanent and debilitating effects, as this causes the bacteria to proliferate. She then went on to see three spine specialists because each diagnosed her with acute pain and suggested an injection; when she said she couldn't have this, they had no other advice and she was forced to move on. Interestingly, Lynn didn't bother to Ask for guidance on finding a spine doctor until she realized that her own efforts weren't working out. When she finally Asked for help, she saw a surgeon who noticed a cyst on her MRI that all the other doctors missed! Once Lynn had the cyst removed, she felt amazing and pursued her Lyme treatment from a place of strength. Lynn's Team influenced how this process played out. Had Lynn seen an orthopedist first, he'd have prescribed steroids, and her Lyme disease would have become much worse. And because she had to keep looking for a specialist who didn't administer steroids, she found a great surgeon who saw the cyst that the other doctors didn't.

As you Ask and listen for health-related answers, be careful not to confuse Spirit's nudges with your own fearful thoughts. This is always true when navigating blocks, but it may feel harder to tell the difference when you're afraid of how an illness might physically progress. Fear may cause you to give yourself a scary WebMD diagnosis before you've seen an expert, second-guess a doctor's point of view, or leap to see a practitioner who's available even if your instincts would warn you to hold off if you gave yourself a chance to listen. Yet when you're listening to your intuition about health direction, the process will carefully unfold before your eyes as you Ask to be shown your next steps. You'll feel a healthy sense of urgency that shows you're serious about your well-being, but not a sense of dire anxiety that causes you to jump to conclusions or make hasty decisions.

Your Turn

In this exercise, you're going to place a request to sustain your health, receive medical guidance, or get healing intervention. You don't need to have a chronic disease or feel deathly ill to do this. Health concerns don't need to be dire to block you. Perhaps you have a tennis elbow that kicks in when it rains or a stubborn virus that won't seem to go away for good. You can only benefit from healing these issues.

Call on a healing angel or guide known for being a health-savvy soul. These include Archangel Raphael, Padre Pio, Native American medicine men, the Buddhist deity Parnashavari, and the Hebrew goddess Asherah. Remember, you can always call on your highest angels and guides if you prefer.

Good health is a major priority to your Team no matter what shape you're in, so I've channeled three requests that should cut across all needs. Feel free, of course, to elaborate on these or simply use them as inspiration. After you've presented your request(s) to Spirit, continue to Ask new questions if your process is ongoing. So if you feel led to try a new diet or exercise regimen, you might later Ask questions like *What program or discipline is good for me? Am I pushing myself too hard or too little?* If you've been guided to one doctor but wonder about a second opinion, consider Asking, *Is this the only practitioner I need to see? Do I feel good about my treatment plan? What other modalities might help me?* What you sense will lead to progress, even if it's to rule things out or confirm what you were already thinking.

Take a few deep breaths to relax. Ground and protect yourself, and Ask a healing soul to join you. For all of the requests below, begin with this intention: "It is my will to maintain my body in good health using God's light and love for myself." Then choose the request most pertinent to your health at this time.

Request to Sustain or Improve Your Health

"With gratitude, I ask to be guided toward the best means of assistance that will help me improve my physical, emotional, and spiritual well-being. Help me to trust and Act on what my Team shows me."

Request for Medical Guidance

"With gratitude, I ask for clear, obvious, and consistent guidance toward practitioners who can help me heal in conjunction with God's energy. Help me to trust and Act on what my Team shows me."

Request for Healing

Though this chapter focuses on physical ailments, a request for healing can be used for emotional, spiritual, and mental impairments, too. Begin with the request "I ask God and all His healing angels to use their loving and healing light to help heal my [name condition here]." Then sit in a chair with your feet on the ground, palms facing up, and picture the healing soul you chose standing before you. Ask this spirit to bathe the areas of your body that need it in healing light and have faith that you're being renewed. As a result, you may find that your fingers tingle, your hands pulse, or you feel warm in the areas you requested. Don't question or doubt that this is the universe's energy; allow the healing to take place.

Act

Spirit says you must exhaust every measure to maintain a healthy body or heal an ill one. So many of us take our physical bodies for granted, but they serve too many purposes to be allowed to fall by the wayside. "Your body is for you to *use*," my guides say. "To make you feel empowered, feel good, feel one with the universe and earth. To allow your energy to blend with all there is, your body must be in a healthy state."

As you Act, remember to address all three bodies when you're ill—physical, mental, and spiritual. I've had clients who were so close to good physical health but couldn't feel truly well until they improved their marriages, discovered a faith that spoke to their souls, or confessed a secret they were harboring. I suggest that once you feel in command of your physical process first—maybe you are comfortable with your treatments or have hit your stride in a new workout—you can then begin to put your mental/emotional and spiritual bodies in order. Find a therapist, schedule a standing lunch date with friends, or join a book club for your mental/emotional bodies. Consider meditating, attending church, or climbing a mountain for your spiritual body. If you're good at multitasking, you can do these while waiting for doctors to call back or test results to come in. Just be sure that all your bodies' needs don't pile up at once and overwhelm you.

Avoiding negativity, heaviness, guilt, and depression while Acting to release health blocks is imperative—whether the gunk belongs to you or someone else. We know that germs contribute to toxic environments, but Spirit says that surrounding yourself with negative people when you're sick is like jumping into a petri dish of psychic bacteria. My client Ed had such severe gastroesophageal reflux disease (GERD) that he was often up all night, choking, coughing, and feeling short of breath because his stomach acid irritated his esophagus and throat. Ed's doctor put him on meds, suggested dietary and sleep changes, and monitored a hiatal hernia. Around the same time, however, Ed was also trying to leave a toxic work environment and fighting terribly with his parents. Everywhere he turned, he felt attacked.

Spirit suggested that Ed use Believe, Ask, and Act to supplement his doctor's orders; Ed's GERD wasn't just a mechanical issue but was actually linked to an ailing mental/emotional body. When it came time for him to Act, Ed was led to look for a new job and have weekly heart-to-hearts with his family. It wasn't until he repaired these areas of his life that Ed saw dramatic health improvements. Eventually he was able to go off all meds and quiet his GERD with diet, lifestyle, and environmental changes alone.

Most of my clients find that the hardest part about Act can be accepting that the path to good health reveals itself as it unfolds. You never know the next step until you take the prior one. Your actions are demonstrations of faith, and it's essential to not let anticipatory anxiety get the best of you. Instead, Act with the trust that your Team is one step ahead of you, because they often are. My client Kimya, for instance, was experiencing strange neurological sensations like numbness, double vision, and brain fog. She'd seen her internist for initial tests and decided that no matter what, she'd also find a good nutritionist for complementary care. Kimya remembered that her agent represented a rather famous one, so she asked if she could contact the woman for a referral in her area. Kimya never told either woman about her specific neurological symptoms, yet as it turned out, the nutritionist sent her an e-mail with this reply: "I'm sorry, I don't know any good nutritionists near you, but I know a fabulous neurologist if you ever need one!" Kimya was floored. Her Team had already begun to put ducks in a row, suspecting her next steps.

Guiding your body to optimal health is a combined effort between you and your Team, but I need you to know that miraculous healings do occur, too. They're the result of earnest faith, ardent prayer, and God's will. They can occur on your own, via prayer chains, or with a healer. Spirit won't tell me why only some of us win the spiritual lottery, but in lieu of this, the three steps are your next best thing.

Your Turn

No matter where your Act process takes you, Spirit encourages you to try this exercise for a healing boost. Once a week, do one *supplemental* activity that focuses on healing your mind, body, or soul—in other words, seeing your doctor or showing up for a weekly acupuncture appointment doesn't count! This could be as indulgent as an hourlong massage, as practical as eating a cup of yogurt to aid with digestion, or as spiritual as reading a series of healing affirmations before bed. In every case, these activities should feel nourishing, beneficial, and sustaining as you strive to live your healthiest life.

CHAPTER 11

Survive Life's Twisters

I magine that a family friend just died, you're in a real estate crisis, and you're facing managerial changes at work, all while dealing with mounting credit card bills that have no end in sight. Stop the madness, right? You might feel cursed or half-jokingly wonder if you've annoyed the gods. The truth is that sometimes "life happens" (to put it nicely) and catalysts are out of your hands. We're spiritual souls in human bodies, living a human existence—challenges come with the territory. The key is to navigate your way out of the natural disaster before it destroys everything in its wake, including your spirit.

When external chaos becomes overwhelming, my Team shows me a swirling tornado. I can actually see a violent cloud spinning around the client I'm reading. I think this sign is so accurate because a real tornado forms when different types of air come together in a specific way; and in Spirit's tornadoes, multiple situations come together to create your life's unstable conditions. When you're blocked by a tornado, the forces working against you are rarely self-inflicted or created by God or Spirit, though you may feel angry, incapable, or defeated from trying to control too much at once. And while some tornadoes can be positive (like when a bride plans a wedding while she's at a busy job), negative whirlwinds are the hardest to manage because there's no clear end point in sight. It takes a greater leap of faith to get there.

Spirit says that your ability to move through multiple obstacles is a spiritual feat that demonstrates faith, endurance, patience, and accountability. It's easy to surrender to a tornado and just hope that it will eventually settle down, but this isn't your best tactic. Standing still is a sign of slipping into denial, and unlike a real tornado, the torrent doesn't pass if you just wait for the storm to blow over. It's also futile to try to outrun a tornado block. When left to their own devices, they pick up speed and wreak more havoc. Instead, your Team wants you to level the chaos and angst because the right response can steer you out of trouble and lead to learning. You'll feel good about how much you can handle if you ever encounter a violent storm again. You'll think, *I made it through that other tornado, so this one will be a breeze.*

Spirit hates tornado blocks as much as you do, so they do their best to help you emerge with your hair and your sanity in place. You're a worldly being, and your Team cannot control what causes every pain and obstacle on this plane, much less five of them clobbering you at once. This reminds me of my friend Tom, who was having problems in his marriage, navigating his son's newly diagnosed learning disability, and scrambling to save his own business—all at the same time. It took Tom about a year to follow his Team's guidance, which included getting his son the right therapies to help him and filing for divorce from his wife. The last time I saw Tom, he was making financial adjustments to get his business back on track. Although some of Tom's stepping-stones were painful, he trusted his faith to guide him toward his next steps throughout and soon he will arrive in a better place.

Free will, impromptu decisions, and bodily imperfections are just a few catalysts for a tornado block—and as you might guess, most are out of Spirit's hands. Your Team can, however, guide you to safety as best as your situation allows. They can prompt a friend to call with a great referral, rearrange a schedule, or nudge you to read a blog that illuminates your next steps. Regardless, you must always investigate the opportunities put in front of you. They rarely offer a shortcut to the Answer, but they *always* help with decision-making in some way.

A tornado of blocks only loses steam when you dismantle it one problem at a time. So what issue do you tackle first? Spirit says to identify and then eliminate the "eye of the storm"—that is, a problem wreaking the most damage and one that, if resolved, will make you feel happiest and initiate the most change across the board. So if money concerns are one of your blocks and trading in a fancy car for a more practical one makes the biggest dent in your finances, which will then affect your mood and ability to pay other expensive bills, that's your best first goal. Or if a health issue keeps you from having a strong mind and temperament to clear other blocks from your whirlwind, fix that one first. See how this works? Then, as you take control and make progress, you break the tornado's energy flow and feel encouraged to keep going. Each step feels more manageable than the ones that preceded it. What's more, Spirit emphasizes that changing your energy from frantic to relative calm allows you to more clearly hear your Team's messages, which is essential for powering through a tornado with purpose, speed, and efficiency.

My client Leslie always has a lot going on, and while she's a practicing Buddhist who does her best to have faith in the universe's opportunities, she is often intimidated about pulling the trigger on them and gets stuck. So when a tornado struck—raining down career choices, family obligations, and money issues, all of which needed immediate resolution—Leslie called on her Team for help. She identified the eye of her storm as her career question, which fed other stress and inertia. Leslie's specific obstacle was whether to accept a transfer to another office or ask for a promotion where she was, since both offered more money and opportunity. After connecting with her Team, Leslie realized that if she did relocate, she'd spend more time at work, and the anxiety she felt around family obligations would intensify. She decided to ask for the promotion, which her boss gladly gave her. Removing this obstacle from Leslie's tornado helped her navigate her other challenges and prevent similar hurdles in the future.

The potentially confusing aspect of a tornado block is that because you're bombarded with so many obstacles at once, it feels like you're being spiritually mega-blocked—*but you're not.* You feel completely overwhelmed, confused, indecisive, and anxiety ridden. A lack of decision-making puts you at a standstill, and it feels as if you'll never see blue skies again. But your Team desperately wants to help you through and is there to help you disable the tornado. They will help you calm the storm so you can think and behave with clarity.

More than with other blocks, Spirit tells me your Team may guide you to multiple possibilities per obstacle that are yours to choose from and Act on. Your happiness is really at stake here and rather immediately, so only you can determine the order in which to address your needs and wants. Free-will choices will steer your direction, and Spirit can't determine those for you. The good news is that using your instincts during a tornado is baptism by fire. You become very familiar with how to quickly hear and respond to your instincts because, frankly, you have no other proactive choice. "A tornado is a huge team effort between you and Spirit," my guides say. "You have to dig deep, focus on a positive end, and navigate out of the storm."

In this chapter, I'll explain what you must spiritually understand to navigate a tornado, how to use your Team to rally support, and how to make it out in one piece.

Believe

- Believe that God or Spirit did not create a whirling dervish to test or punish you, and there is no such thing as a cosmic black cloud. These are distorted views of God's and the universe's priorities. Your Team cares about every aspect of your life, but they don't control every aspect of the world you live in. Know, too, that you're not attracting an onslaught of negativity. Rather, a tornado is the very definition of "when it rains, it pours." God created free will and cause and effect, and most of life's circumstances and decisions are based on your choices and that of others; happenstance is what causes them to collide at once. So don't live in fear of the tornado God might bestow; live in awe of the opportunities He'll provide to get you out of its grip.

- Believe that God wants you to use your worldly and spiritual resources to ground your twister. You can pray all you want for better finances, but if you ignore the accountant that your Team sends your way, you are ignoring the universe's direction and thus sabotaging your efforts. Be careful that in the midst of a tornado, you don't become disconnected from your inner voice or Spirit's cues. Believe that your Team wants you to use these moments productively and will continue to provide signs to direct your next steps.

- Believe there will be positive moments during your trials (I promise!), and express gratitude when you feel those moments. It might be when you receive a sign or can check an item off your to-do list, bringing you closer to overcoming an obstacle. Maybe you've learned there is an answer to a situation that at one time felt hopeless or there's a reason for what once felt like an unanswered prayer. For every door that opens and every request that's addressed, say thanks. Gradually, a more positive outlook will buoy your process.

This makes me think of my client Paige, who was in the midst of a tornado that involved learning to balance the demands of her new baby with a busy career, caring for her perpetually sick dog, and figuring out how to resolve painful migraines related to a neck injury. She chose, as her first block, to find a way to treat her headaches so that she could think clearly and navigate her other problems. During church one Sunday, she prayed that her angels direct her to a unanimous solution—be it meds, Botox injections, acupuncture, or another modality. A few days later, her friend Emily popped into her head when she was thinking about her situation, so she sent her a quick text asking if she'd ever dealt with neck-related headaches. Why not ask, right? Turns out, Emily had and suggested a local chiropractor. A *chiropractor? I had no idea,* Paige thought. *Thank you for the idea, God.* Paige was so appreciative because Emily's idea felt like a blessed lead, especially since she didn't have the energy or time to weed through opinions and explore dead-end options. A few hours later, Paige then ran into her daughter's teacher at the store. She remembered that this woman struggled with severe headaches, too. Paige asked how she was feeling, and the teacher praised *her* chiropractor, who also does Reiki healings. *Another chiro! This is more than a coincidence*, Paige thought. She marveled at the universe's consistency and felt incredibly grateful that she was closer to a specific and promising answer. That same night, Paige called her mom to say hi, and before she could tell her about the flurry of serendipitous insight, her mother announced, "I just saw this crazy news segment on something called Network Spinal Analysis. It's a new kind of chiropractic treatment. . . . " This time, Paige laughed and said aloud to her Team, "Message received, loud and clear, guys! Thanks!" While a chiropractor wasn't initially on her radar, Paige now had multiple divinely sent options, and it was up to her to find the best fit. So much reinforcement actually made her excited to investigate the practitioners she'd heard about, which is far from the attitude she had about her headaches to this point. Paige felt unwavering faith that whatever treatment she chose, her Team would guide her toward a positive end.

Your Turn

Affirm your belief that you can survive a twister by thinking or saying, "I Believe Spirit will give me the clarity to envision a positive outcome and endurance to power through any storm."

Ask

As you seek to ground a tornado, you may find yourself Asking for more direction than with other blocks because you're muscling through multiple scenarios, one after another after another. The Ask questions in the following "Your Turn" section will direct you to Act, but as you move through each day, you may want to Ask follow-up questions that help you make mini-choices if you're stuck. *Which highway will get me to my appointment fastest? Who can watch the kids while I'm putting out fires? Will having drinks with this friend add to my mood right now?* You'll receive rapid-fire answers from your Team, and by the time you're almost through your block, you may even be able to Act on instinct without Asking so much to prompt it. You'll just feel the right direction in which to head, and you'll find that it works out nicely.

My friend Shelby got swept up in a tornado, and I love how she survived it using the three steps even though she'd never tried this technique before. Within a two-week window, Shelby went to contract on a new home, she found out she needed to support her mom through a surgery, her boss moved up the deadline on a project, and Shelby found a lump on her son's leg that needed a specialist's opinion. As each scenario and its responsibilities piled on top of Shelby, her thoughts raced and stomach clenched. She worried about thoughtfully jumping all these hurdles.

Because time was of the essence, Shelby practiced Believe and Ask rather quickly. She affirmed her belief with the statement I suggested earlier, then used the Ask questions in "Your Turn" to receive instant replies. Her strategy was to think through all the pieces of the tornado first, get her priorities in order, and then start taking action. She didn't have a drawn-out conversation with her Team. Her first talk with Spirit went like this:

What's my priority?

Get your son to the doctor.

How will this help other situations in my life?

You won't be able to focus, knowing his health hangs in the balance.

What resources will logistically help me the most?

Support from husband and babysitter always on call.

What's my next step?

Only plan three days ahead—more will overwhelm you.

With a general game plan in mind, Shelby then moved to her second priority: mom's surgery. She Asked the same four questions she did for her son's obstacle and listened for answers. She then repeated this step until she'd accounted for all the challenges in her tornado. Shelby did all of this over the course of a week, and if she hit a wall with any detail of her plan, she simply Asked the questions again. She didn't have time to deliberate on what she heard at any point, which means she listened to her purest instincts. Once she knew how to work through all four obstacles, she Acted on them one at a time, waiting for each to feel relatively manageable before moving on to the next. After four months, Shelby's tornado had settled.

Your Turn

If you are in a tornado block right now, this is your lucky day (yes, really). I'd like you to use your situation for this exercise. If you aren't in one, you can use your to-do list for the week or month instead.

Spirit says to call on an abundance of angels for this Ask, so fill your mind's eye to its capacity with as many beautifully lit beings as you can envision. To me, angels can appear as colors, some have wings, and all are silhouettes that radiate glorious light, but they should fit your frame of reference.

In meditation or during prayer, picture your obstacles as words swirling around you—like "work travel," "hip pain," "school play rehearsal," and "sick dog"—and then take a deep breath and Ask your angels for help. Grab at the word that is your top priority, and then Ask the four questions below.

To order your future priorities, imagine grabbing other words, one at a time. Ask your Team the four questions for those, too. This will establish a few useful basics for navigating out of the tornado.

When you are ready, visualize your beautiful angels and state this intention: "I commit to envisioning the positive outcome that I know I can create. I will do this by paying attention to where my divine Team is guiding me. I commit to discovering the action that guides me to my answers." Then calmly Ask the questions, listen for answers, and thank your Team for their help.

Four Questions

What is my priority?

How will this help other situations in my life?

What resource will logistically help me the most? What is a reliable backup?

What's my next step?

Act

As you Act, Spirit implores you to not get in your own way. A tornado is complicated enough; you don't have the time or energy to create another block! If people do get in their own way, this mostly happens via self-sabotage, blaming others, or not taking responsibility for their choices. At the core of getting in your own way is an unwillingness to take chances, step outside your comfort zone, and claim responsibility for your choices. You will not clear an iota of chaos if you introduce a negative mind-set. Use the energy you'd exert making excuses or dodging responsibility to focus on what you *can* do to create positive change.

You'll notice that the energy behind your Act steps echoes traits known to generally breed success: discipline, confidence, an ability to ask for help, a determination to not overthink, gratitude for your growth. Would you rather feel defeated as the storm around you grows stronger? No way. My client Lori was freaking out about the tornado sweeping through her life—a toxic relationship growing nastier, studying for finals her senior year of college, and a full-time job as a hairdresser. Lori felt pulled in too many directions, was unfocused on doing any one thing well, and wanted to hide under the covers from it all.

Yet when I helped Lori use the three steps to navigate her tornado, her Act process was inspiring! In fact, she exercised a sense of authority, guts, and structure that business students know well. The first thing Lori did was "fire" her boyfriend, which momentarily made her tornado more tumultuous because she now had to deal with heartache and disappointment, too. She could, however, focus better on studying for finals and staying later at the salon since she didn't have to meet up with him after work. Lori considered a move to Florida after graduation, but she realized this was an idea that had come from her mind as a way of running from her life. She admitted to me that fear had no place in the next chapter of her life, so she'd replace it with bravado. Lori stayed put, and she's now researching investors to help her purchase the salon she works in. She is holding on tight to a thriving relationship with a wonderful new boyfriend. She's so happy, it's ridiculous.

Your Turn

Your Act steps will be directly influenced by what you felt during Ask, but I channeled a meditation exercise to help you further determine next steps if you ever feel frustrated and stalled. Breathe in and out a few times with your eyes shut. Picture yourself in a dark room and, in the distance, visualize a word in front of you that represents the obstacle you're conquering at this moment. Then, visualize a door on either side of the word, one with a green light and one with a red light above it. Open the door with the red light to reveal an image related to your next step that you should *avoid*; open the door with the green light to reveal an image related to your next step that you should *follow*. Trust that your Universal Team presented you with these visuals and opportunities, and fold them into your Act process.

CHAPTER 12

Leave Your Comfort Zone Behind

"Step out of your comfort zone" might sound more like a business coach's priority than God's, but your Universal Team often asks me to channel this very message; at its core is an actionable, spiritual tenet. After all, if you want to release the blocks that keep you from happiness, you have to be willing to take chances that guide you there. And even when those efforts feel uncomfortable, your Team will always steer and support them. Spirit's whole purpose is to help you create the kind of powerful positivity that arises when dreams come to fruition. Have faith that with God and your Team's guidance, the unknown is awesome. Put your hesitations aside, believe in your own gifts and instincts, and trust in the process.

When Spirit wants to encourage my clients to expand their horizons, they show me a symbol that I'm sure you've seen on Pinterest memes and motivational posters from the '80s. It's a circle with a dot inside it that's labeled "Your Comfort Zone," and then there's a second dot outside the circle with the words "Where the magic happens." When Spirit shows me this sign, they want me to convey how essential it is for my clients to push their boundaries and take healthy chances. The sign typically arises when clients are either considering or at the start of a major decision that's exciting but also gives them pause, such as a job change, geographical move, a new relationship or commitment of some kind, and the like. From Spirit's perspective, stepping outside your comfort zone means taking an adventurous leap of faith and enjoying the process; it's a very positive symbol for me. You may feel some trepidation, but it's more of a thrilling, nail-biting nervousness that motivates you toward a positive outcome rather than a negative or suffocating fear that hampers your happiness. Anticipating the steps to your destination should also feel exhilarating, not laborious or terrifying. In fact, Spirit says this kind of emotional rush is a sign that you're on the cusp of growth.

Since it can be challenging to immediately start from a place of yes, Spirit says it's just as productive to begin with the question "What if I did?" This causes you to visualize a thoughtful, in-your-wildest-dreams answer that your Team can use as a reference point when presenting opportunities that align with your hopes. After all, the universe wants you to enjoy rolling the dice and do it often. I love a poem called "The Dash" by Linda Ellis, and in it she says, "What matters is how we live and love/and how we spend our dash"—meaning the years represented by a dash on your tombstone between the year you're born and the year you die. Spirit says you're meant to take positive risks that speak to you, or you'll always question whether you're fulfilling your potential or missing out on life. That's no way to spend your dash.

Comfort zone activities that you want to avoid are those that compromise who you are or ask you to hold on to habits and routines that lead to disappointment or sadness—frankly, anything that occurs at the expense of growth, learning, and joy. As you might guess, stagnant choices cause roadblocks to happiness and inner satisfaction. In fact, when Spirit hears clients say, "I feel like a gerbil on a wheel," "I feel like I'm missing out," or "I'm on a path to nowhere," they downright insist that you shake things up. Change your focus to change your energy. Go back to school, train for a marathon, or take a road trip. You don't want to go so far outside of your zone that you feel like you've just walked off a cliff, but you should feel exhilarated, heightened, challenged, and very excited. You don't have to be a thrill seeker to push your limits, either. Your soul lightens just as much when you cook an exotic meal as when you jump out of a plane if both stimulate you in fresh ways. I've found that your Team is behind whatever will make you happy, as long as it comes from a pure place and doesn't hurt others. The subsequent positivity feeds your soul, inspires you to spread the joy to those around you, and sends out a positive vibration from you and them that helps the universe.

Spirit suggests that each time you Act with an encouraging step, you take a moment to realize *I'm okay* and then take another step. You'll feel increasingly brave and aware that when you face new mountains, you'll climb them, too. When I began reading clients, it was very hard for me to "come out" to friends as a medium, even though I was excited that I'd honed this awesome ability. I've always feared judgment, and I didn't want the people closest to me to misinterpret the situation and turn away. I was nervous they'd think I was a bad Catholic or liked talking to the dead in a creepy manner. But after I told one person, she was fine with it, and so I felt okay to tell another, and another . . . and these days, I can't *stop* my friends from asking me to use my gift to help them! Mindfully expanding my comfort zone has helped me become who I am. In fact, when my son's friend told him that "[psychics] like your mom are full of it," my knee-jerk reaction wasn't to drive over to this kid's house and give him a beat-down. Instead, I said that it doesn't matter what others think, and I meant it. The teaching moment was really validating for me. I helped my son see that the more you stand behind your beliefs, the less you need others to substantiate them.

Not surprisingly, stepping outside your comfort zone helps align you with your best path. Your imprint is composed of hopes and adventures, both pursued and deferred, and Spirit doesn't want you to compromise or sacrifice in a way that eats at your soul's identity. This reminds me of my client John, who came to me so we could connect with his deceased father. Right away, Dad's soul stepped forward and placed a ceiling just above John's head. When Spirit does this to a client, it's a symbol to show me that the person is preventing himself from growth because he's too comfortable. John's father, a vocal member of his son's Team, then told me that while John was in nursing school, he secretly dreamed of becoming a doctor. "You have the potential, and you know you can do this," I channeled.

He showed me that being a doctor would more closely align John with his imprint. I suggested John use the three steps to encourage his Team to place opportunities in his path for him to grab or ignore; and if he pursued them with pure intentions, hard work, and persistence, he'd come out on top. When I last saw John, he'd changed his major to premed and was studying to be an oncologist. "It's easy to forget the human will is tenacious and what you are all capable of doing," my guides say. "Your life is not as confined as you make it."

It's been my experience that when we step outside our comfort zones, our spirits rise to the occasion. In this chapter, I'll focus on how you can work in conjunction with God and your Team to reach goals that live "where the magic happens." I'll share the beliefs that will support you during this process, explain how to request clear direction en route, and channel tips that will help you reach the finish line.

Believe

- Believe that stepping out of your comfort zone lightens and brightens your energy for your soul's enrichment and the universal good. And while your angels and guides are excited for you to feel the euphoria that comes with taking leaps of faith, Believe there is a higher reason for their guidance, too. It's your Team's job to care, because you are part of a system that powers the universe; and as your teachers, your Team will do everything they can to help you learn and achieve to enhance your soul for you and the greater good. The lighter your energy, the faster you move to new levels and the more powerful the universe becomes. Spirit says we are all born with a duty to live as our truest self, and it's within that form that we achieve our personal greatness. Stepping out of your comfort zone and toward an exciting new future is a service not only to yourself but to the whole universe.

- Believe that as you take chances, your Team will offer you support and tools to relieve the discomfort that comes with uncertainty. This may arrive as a peaceful sensation that washes over you when you're thinking about the task at hand, a sense of knowing and awareness that you're being guided, or signs from your departed loved ones. This last one happened when my son stepped out of his comfort zone. I encouraged him to play a sport and suggested he ask God and his Team for help determining his best choice, since he was worried about juggling the responsibilities of being an athlete and managing his academics at the same time. A week later, he announced that after much consideration, he'd decided to play football. Cut to a few weeks into the season, when I heard him humming the song "Eye of the Tiger." This made me laugh because it's a song that my spirit guides sing to me when I'm meant to empower a client! I asked my son where he'd heard it, and he said, "I don't know; it just popped into my head." I told him, "That's your sign—for both of us—that you made the right choice. Hum it as your mantra!" He's doing great as an offensive lineman and feels really good about himself on the field.

- Believe, too, that worthwhile pursuits don't exist *only* outside your comfort zone. You may have different comfort zones for different areas of your life, and when you're happily "in the zone" for any of them, that elevates your soul, too. I'm comfortable with my role as a mother and feel no need to take a risk there; ditto for my marriage. I feel content and stimulated, the love flows freely, and I feel safe being myself. I'm in my groove, and these corners of my world natu-rally click. Thus, they're innately positive comfort zones for me because I'm at my best.

- Believe that if you set a goal and hit a wall in its pursuit, this is sim-ply a detour and not an early end point; your journey may be longer than you wish, but it's never meant to stop short of your goal.
    This point comes up a lot when ambitious clients expect to

climb the career ladder at an unrealistically fast pace that ultimately won't serve them. My client Terry, for instance, works as a bank teller and has stepped outside her comfort zone in an effort to become a Reiki Master. So Terry began taking classes, but she'd only been training for a few months when she asked me when she'd have a thriving practice! I then saw that she felt discouraged that lately her healings had become less accurate, and her Team said they'd blocked her in this way so that she'd focus, savor, and fine-tune her skills rather than get ahead of herself. Terry's detour was simply a teaching moment. Remember, Spirit has a plan and needs you to see it through. Reflect on the factors during this process that have made you feel good, tweak your approach based on what's working, and be sure to take in any lessons you've learned along the way. Perhaps you received constructive criticism, grew a thicker skin, and now are more open to others' perspectives. You're not just turning lemons into limonata or placating yourself by thinking there's a reason you're derailed. Use your lessons as signposts to help you get back on track.

Your Turn

Affirm your belief that you can leave your comfort zone behind by thinking or saying, "I Believe that my heart is strong, my will is tough, and God will provide me with all that's enough."

Ask

Ask will help you expand the boundaries of who you are and what you want your life to be. As you push the edges of your comfort zone, you'll continue to broaden this space to include new experiences and roles that fulfill you. Eventually, the magic won't happen outside these limits but within your life every day.

As you Ask, be sure to establish and maintain realistic expectations for who you are right now. Don't limit your dreams, but also don't set your sights on grandiose goals like winning the lottery or pursuing aims that are completely out of your control or downright impractical—and certainly not overnight. My client Sarah, for example, has thrived because of her realistic attempts to jump outside her comfort zone. Sarah is a smart and friendly college student who was once crippled with anxiety that turned her into a painful introvert. When I first read her, Spirit showed me that Sarah rarely went out, constantly self-criticized, and stuck to summer jobs like babysitting so she didn't have to interact with others her age. Yet Sarah wanted to be and do more, and when she got to college, she decided to study in Spain for a semester with strangers from all over the world. She embraced a new situation that challenged her but within the safety of a school program. She would have set herself up for trouble had she chosen to, say, quit college and move alone to the Congo.

Praying to her angels, Sarah focused on Asking three questions: *Is this right for me? Will I make friends? Will I be okay?* After each one, she felt a calm and clear "Yes." She bought her ticket, had a blast abroad, and stays in touch with a group of friends she met in Europe. It was such a life-changer that Sarah returned to her home college more confident than when she left, and she plans to teach in Spain after graduation.

As Spirit guides you through the Ask process, you may feel a bit like a snake that's slowly shedding its skin. When a snake grows and eventually reaches a point where further growth in its current skin isn't possible, a new layer of skin grows under the current one, and the old skin peels off. As you Ask questions that guide you outside your comfort zone, you'll learn to slip right out of the routines and habits that are no longer useful to you. You will become one with the "new skin" you've grown, and you'll feel proud of the person the world sees. Spirit says this response isn't ego, by the way. It's empowerment and hard-earned pride for your newfound capabilities.

Your Turn

I'd like you to work on a goal outside your comfort zone that makes you feel nervously excited and then use Ask to achieve it. For instance, you may want to get over your stage fright when speaking in public, take a break from dating after years of relationships, or train for a marathon. This goal may or may not be blocking you, but you can only benefit from pursuing passions that reflect your soul. My guides suggest that you do this Ask exercise in three parts over the course of three days. The process will help you crystallize your vision, feel supported, and take next steps.

For Part I, you will choose a well-intentioned, realistic goal. Remember to establish expectations that your Team can work with and you can rely on. Don't presume that as a college grad, the three steps will help you become an overnight Fortune 500 prodigy. Not. Gonna. Happen. Also remember that your timelines and outcome may be colored by your Team's lessons for you and others involved. Your request may not be met exactly how you'd hoped, so stay open to Spirit's solutions as you encounter them.

For Part II, Ask your Team to support your goal in a positive light. This creates a great foundation that you can return to for encouragement as you pursue the goal. I find that the hardest part of trying new things is that the smallest hesitation can feel like a major sticking point, since everything about the situation—from what you feel to how you're behaving—is unfamiliar. It's easier to give up than find an alternate path. Choose your mode of encouragement based on what you need at that moment. One comforting way to receive encouragement is to Ask that you feel your guides at work. You can invite this in a quick, casual way ("Thank you for surrounding me"). You can also Ask to receive signs from your loved ones that they're with you, knowing this may not happen instantaneously ("I'm open to receiving the signs you provide"). I like to Ask guides for a pep talk, voice of reason, or extra encouragement and motivation when I need it. As I mentioned in Chapter 4, Spirit will respond to you in the third person—something like "You can do anything you put your mind to" or "You're in your element." I also Ask for reassurance in channeled writings from my angels and guides because it offers immediate gratification. And if your uneasiness feels too overwhelming for an exercise? Ask your Team to take the feeling away by saying, "Thank you for removing my jitters so I can think and act clearly."

In Part III, Ask your Team how to take your first step toward your goal. Prepare for a tiptoe or leap—there's no telling what Spirit has in store, so it's key to remain flexible and aware. For reassurance, you may even want to visualize yourself in the comfort zone symbol I described earlier, standing on the edge of the circle and diving off the edge as if you're plunging into a cool, refreshing swimming pool.

Heading into uncharted waters requires dynamic energy, so my guides offered two types of powerhouse energy for this. First, you can request the soul of a departed family member who embodied adventure and encouragement while they were alive. This presence should also make you feel that you're being held accountable for your actions and follow-through. Brassy Italian and Jewish grandmothers come to mind! Your other option is to Ask for guidance based on the energy you crave. You can do this by drawing attention to your third chakra, also called your Solar Plexus, located in the center of your upper abdomen. This chakra is associated with fire and the power of transformation; it's the center of willpower and achievement. Every chakra in your body is associated with a color, and for me, this one is yellow. To channel energy from your Solar Plexus, close your eyes and visualize yellow light around and within you. Then Ask God to send you a soul that will help you reach this chakra's fullest potential.

When you're ready to begin, take a moment to quiet, ground, and protect yourself, then call on the soul that best resonates with you. State the intention: "I commit to having the strength to become all that God has intended me to be." Then Ask, stay open, and express gratitude for your guidance.

Part I

What would you like to do outside your comfort zone?

How does this opportunity make you feel?

How would this change your daily life?

How will it help you become your truest self?

Part II

Ask for your Team's support now and whenever you need it. This is always beneficial if your goal feels stalled, you're nervous or afraid, or you've hit a dead end. My guides suggest two great ways to do this.

For comforting pep talks, I like to do channeled writings. Here, write a question at the top of the page that reflects what's on your mind, such as "What am I missing?" or "What am I worried about?" Then let the answers flow from within you without hesitation or judgment.

Another effective, supportive technique is to Ask Spirit to remind you of a time when you stepped out of your comfort zone and your life soared as a result. Think about the feelings and steps it took to get you there, how you could have potentially bypassed roadblocks if you'd paid more attention to your instincts sooner, and how it felt to reach the finish line. Hold on to that final feeling because that is what you're meant to feel every time you push your boundaries in a way that aligns with your soul's path. Return to it when you need to be reminded of how gratifying the end result will feel.

Part III

Is this a good time to take a leap of faith?

If not, when might it be?

If yes, how should I set up my time frame?

How do I take the next step?

Act

During Act, be sure your intentions remain clear, pure, and honest as you demonstrate them. When you step outside your comfort zone, it's easy to get caught up in the excitement that comes with new experiences. "Consider why you're taking the positive risk and how it will benefit others," my guides suggest. My client Jeremy flipped houses as a side business, and when he first began, he put his heart into turning architectural trash into saleable treasures that made other people happy. Yet as Jeremy made more and more money from his homes, his intentions became convoluted. He began to cut corners so he could move at a faster pace and turn over more inventory, and greed took over. With each ego-driven gain, Jeremy grew further from his initial vision. Spirit says his success wasn't the problem; it was the energy he now used to fuel it. Gradually, Jeremy's Team began stalling projects and limiting opportunities, the market declined, and Jeremy's business bottomed out. Though spiritual and worldly factors led to the company's downfall, Spirit didn't help Jeremy rescue his business because his intentions had become convoluted. His Team did, however, guide him to run a property management business, which addressed his real estate interests and need to make a living. In this work, there was less room for him to feel motivated by immediate financial gains.

Spirit listens and responds to thought—in fact, on the Other Side, all soul communication is telepathic—so the way you mentally frame actions as you do them is very important. Stepping outside your comfort zone often requires sacrifice, so it helps to continue to think positively about the big-picture result and not bemoan any smaller steps that pinch. Reduce your struggle by accepting that detours and missteps are bound to happen. Focus, instead, on all the new opportunities and feelings that come with forward motion. When my friend Paula stepped out of her comfort zone by working outside her home for the first time in ten years, she offset her readjustment period by focusing on the perks of this risk—adult conversation, happy hour, free pens. Spirit supports and rewards positive responses to trying situations.

Even so, Spirit tells me one of the most hampering moves you can make is to get *too* stuck in your head during Act. There's a fine balance between creating enthusiastic (positive) and desperate (negative) energy, and you stir up the latter when you become so obsessed with reaching your goal that your efforts are imbalanced. When my client Bella went outside her comfort zone to adopt a baby from Haiti, she took every bird, song, and conversation to be a sign from Spirit, *then* spent hours journaling about potential next steps, *then* asked her friends what they thought she should do, *then* got upset if they didn't agree with her, *then* ignored it all and started over . . . it was a crazy-making Act process that created anxiety. She was so frantic for affirmation that her actions actually demonstrated a lack of trust in Spirit. This lack of trust caused her to panic and made her second-guess herself and her Team. Stepping outside your comfort zone is meant to be fun and exciting and to spread positivity. Despite potential twists and turns, you have to Act with the faith that your guides know what they're doing. You're also more likely to enjoy where you land if you're in the moment as you go.

When you Act with faith, confidence, and courage, your ever-expanding comfort zone offers you a generous space to explore, create, and write your own story. My friend Brandon is a cool example of someone whose life took off when he jumped outside his comfort zone. (Spirit often shows me his story when they want me to talk about comfort zones. Though I hadn't been shown Believe, Ask, and Act at that time, they've since assigned the steps to his process.) For three years, Brandon worked as a train conductor, though it never spoke to his soul. He came from a long line of railroad employees, including his dad, who insisted that job security be his top priority. Yet Brandon's need to strike out on his own persisted.

Brandon knew he wanted to start with a business degree, but he couldn't afford to put himself through school. He had a strong belief system based in positive thought and recited affirmations every morning, so he Asked for guidance during meditation and felt led to chart a timeline for himself—from going to school on the railroad's dime to thinking outside the box when it was time to interview for jobs. When Brandon graduated in the mid-'90s, he heard about a tech start-up that developed and provided Internet ad serving services. It sounded like a positive risk and one that Brandon felt energized to take on.

I assured Brandon that his nervous excitement was a good sign, and he dove into Act mode. He impressed the company during his interview and was hired on the spot. Brandon's gut told him to invest what little money he had into the company. By the late '90s, however, the dot-com world crashed and Brandon's business went under. Naturally, he was upset, but instead of running back to the railroad for guaranteed job security and his father's approval, Brandon decided to keep going. He secured a job with a new but promising tech upstart as a salesman. He felt good and continued to have faith in God; he didn't allow himself to feel deterred and took time off from cynics who fed his fear. Once again, Brandon invested a portion of his earnings in the company. There were times Brandon was legitimately worried about his future, but he'd return to his affirmations and frame the situation in a positive light. Stock drops became an invitation to improve. Management shake-ups were an opportunity for fresh blood. You can imagine how much faith it took to quiet Brandon's rational mind, which told him he was nuts to trust the tech world twice, but he chose to listen to his inner voice that said, *Stay with this*. He never doubted his guidance, and sure enough, he and the company flourished. It's called Google—maybe you've heard of it.

The bonus prize isn't that Brandon's intuition led him to make a lot of money (though it did). It's that the more he pushed his limits, the more rewarding his *entire life* became. Because Brandon succeeded from taking a chance in one area, he had the guts to take chances outside the office. He let go of commitment issues, fell in love, and got married. He made time to strengthen his body, began running marathons, and became an Ironman. Google appreciated Brandon's pep, which reflected their culture. Pushing boundaries fed Brandon's mind, body, and soul. The last time we met, Brandon had left Google and was investing in new companies he believed in. The man is on a roll.

Your Turn

Your Act steps will be determined by what you sensed during Ask, but Spirit thought that charting out your initial steps on a cheerful diagram might lend some clarity. Draw a circle on a piece of paper and label it "My Comfort Zone." Along the inner perimeter, write down the words that represent the duties, relationships, roles, and goals that make you feel safe and low stress—in both good and bad ways. For instance, a sample list might include titles like "wife" and "mother" and a job title that you hope to transition from to better reflect your passions or ambitions. Some will bring calm, happy feelings while others should make you feel nervous excitement. Then, draw one line that extends off each word and write another word or phrase that represents what you believe you could accomplish if you pushed yourself a little further. These should make you smile and your heart beat a little faster in anticipation of what's to come. For instance, the title "wife" might have a line that extends to "date night, twice a month" and the job title "head engineer" might have a line that extends to "president in five years." Some words might already feed your soul, and for those, you can write the words "okay" or "content." By the end of the exercise, you'll have outlined and turned your greatest desires into a literal ray of sunshine.

RADIATING BELIEVE, ASK, and ACT to the WORLD

CHAPTER 13

Know You're Limitless

Most of my clients assume that God has only one road in mind for them, and they can either travel it correctly, which is when it feels "meant to be," or blow it entirely. As I hope I've made very clear by now, that is not the case. God wants you to live in joy, integrity, and connection with the world. It's what you do with all of your blessings, accidents, and disappointments that matters most to your soul and to God. Beautiful miracles will always occur, but they're out of your control. They're God's call and angels' responsibilities to carry out. Everyday life is in the capable hands of you and your Universal Team.

God created your soul to be boundless. You're meant to dream big, accept divine guidance, and overcome great obstacles. Throughout this book, you've practiced Believe, Ask, and Act to release blocks and navigate your life. I hope as you've moved through the book, you have found the process getting easier. Rest assured that as you've worked to hone your ability to receive guidance, your efforts have helped align you with your soul's path. As you continue to surmount obstacles and practice spiritual priorities, you will continue to raise your consciousness and feel in tune with the angels and guides that walk beside you every step of the way. Believing that there are no limits to what you can do means you aren't just listening to and Acting on your Team's advice—it is now one with your soul. Your worldly and heavenly selves are connected, and you are experiencing the best of all planes.

When a client's Team insists that the person is limitless, they show me the glass elevator scene from the original *Charlie and the Chocolate Factory*. Remember when Willy Wonka, Charlie, and Grandpa Joe press the chute's "Up and Out" button, which causes them to burst through the ceiling and soar into the heavens? That's how Spirit feels about your potential to create happiness and change when you listen to your instincts and follow your Universal Team's guidance. Using the three steps can help you master this, and in doing so, you've pressed the spiritual "Up and Out" button that sends you on a thrilling, boundless ride. At one time or another, we have all felt that we were at the universe's fickle mercy—accepting jobs we felt we had to take, dwelling in sadness from situations that seemed thrust upon us for no good reason, wondering if we were destined to always feel blah. But now you know that if you work in conjunction with your Team, you can navigate tough scenarios, affect your soul's journey, and embrace a deeply content life.

Take a moment to pause, reflect, and celebrate how far you've come! This is a very big deal.

WHAT DOES IT MEAN TO BE LIMITLESS?

Before I further explain what Spirit means when they use the term *limitless*, let me first share what limitless is *not*. It is not a state that makes you invincible or exempt from life's curveballs. It does not keep you from getting your heart broken, becoming ill, or feeling down when circumstances go south—you're only human. It's certainly not about manifesting richness or status. And while Believe, Ask, and Act present opportunities that feel magical, it is in no way magic, and Spirit is not your personal Houdini.

On the contrary, limitless souls appreciate that the universe does, in fact, have limits and welcome what their Teams have up their sleeves. My client Roxanne has grown tremendously in the time I've known her, and I would describe her as limitless. When we first met, she frequently complained that the sky was falling and only on her—from where Roxanne sat, *nobody* faced the financial hardships, health problems, and career roller coasters that *she* did. So when Roxanne saw me for a reading and shared that she was having trouble conceiving, I worried about how she might react if I didn't see a baby in her future.

But during Roxanne's session, I saw that she'd raise *two* babies. Roxanne was thrilled with the news because she was undergoing fertility treatments and hoping for twins. Her Team, however, asked her to consider adoption because her body was capable of producing only one biological child; this was a worldly limit that Spirit, for whatever reason, had to work with. Now if I'd channeled this news years before, Roxanne might have plugged her ears and insisted on having the family she'd envisioned, exactly as she'd envisioned it—and when that didn't happen, she likely would have railed against the universe. She'd have kept trying to do things her way rather than accepting the opportunities her Team offered her. However, Roxanne had been using the principles behind Believe, Ask, and Act long enough to know that when she hit a roadblock, her angels would guide her to a solution that spoke to her core desires—in this case, to raise a family. This is exactly what happened when Roxanne began the adoption process while still doing fertility treatments. In a year's time, she'd adopted a son and given birth to a daughter. Roxanne had developed the ability to seek a positive outcome, get out of her own way, and adjust her perspective by listening to her Team and accepting her and Spirit's limits. This allowed her to hear, pursue, and accept God's blessings.

When Spirit uses the term *limitless*, they're referring to your soul's power and the strength of your consciousness. It's about knowing you can always apply your talents, connection to Spirit, and honed intuition to change the areas of your life that make you feel stuck or unhappy. You can also use your limitless nature to enhance the areas that already feel good. Limitless is an internal state that's reflected outward—an ability to endure, pursue, and embody great contentment. It's remembering that you, as a human, are capable of amazing feats because you know how to use the instinctual tools that God gave you and view life through a positive lens. It's recognizing, accepting, and embracing the person you are and want to be.

As a limitless soul, you are acutely aware of how a higher power operates in and around you, because your soul's path is aligned with the universe's limitless abundance. You now know how it feels to work in conjunction with God and his messengers' energy and also against it. You know the importance of a mind, body, and soul connection and, when one element is imbalanced, how to get back to your baseline. It should begin to feel natural to keep moving forward with strength, perspective, and confidence rather than fear or hesitation because you know what to do when you hit a bump in the road or make a wrong turn. It's become easier to speak, behave, and love from a place of strength and action because you know how to respond rather than offhandedly react to conflicts. Even when you face challenges, you feel an awareness and acceptance—not to be confused with resignation—that reflects an elevated soul. It's become your nature to wake up feeling grateful, make an extra effort to help others, and live in a way that feels true.

SHARE YOUR SPIRIT

Now that you know your soul is limitless, find ways to use your higher consciousness to pay it forward on a regular basis in a way that feeds you, others, and the universe. You don't have to do this through huge gestures like building schools for underprivileged kids or saving the elephants of Samburu, Africa. You can show others your limitless soul and what you ultimately value through small efforts, too. Are you a person who shows up late or on time for a family dinner? Can you hold the door open for a stranger instead of stepping through it first? Do you ask a friend about his day before launching into a discussion of yours? Are you a parent who says "I love you" with frequency and heart instead of on an as-needed basis? In every moment and with every belief, feeling, thought, word, and action, you choose to be the person you want to share with the world. You have a choice about whether to respond to and feed your best self or travel a lesser path than the one your soul designed.

You should also share the spiritual priorities you learned about while overcoming blocks using this book, and the best way to do this is to lead by example and model what you have learned. Our greatest purpose and privilege on earth is to serve one another with the love and wisdom we've learned to be true. So if you've discovered that your authentic self loves to cook, make a lasagna to split with the neighbors. If you've learned to coexist with grief, embrace your inner peace and try to help out others going through the same. When you overcome a health issue, live in the moment but also donate some time off to a cause that speaks to your soul. Be gentle, patient, and kind to others because you don't know what their experiences and heartaches are or have been. Every choice you make colors the joy and energy that you feel and give to others. They keep you on a path of happiness and positive motion. As my guides like to say, "Give light to others, and the Light will fill you up."

As I've said before, God and Spirit are not asking you to be perfect—not by any means. It is more than enough to be conscious of where you direct your ongoing energy most often. Your very best choices reflect your limitless soul, who you authentically are, and what's genuinely important to you. Every day, you can either impair your greatness or reach new, unlimited heights like Willy, Charlie, and Grandpa Joe.

USING BELIEVE, ASK, AND ACT EVERY DAY

Believe, Ask, and Act are meant to *empower* you—this is the feeling God wants you to have as you navigate your life's direction. So far, you've used the three steps specifically to overcome obstacles, which has given you tools and experience to positively manage challenges. But this practice has come with an awesome bonus prize. Regularly engaging your Universal Team has awoken your instincts and allowed you to utilize your relationship with them so effectively that you are now primed to use the steps every day and as a matter of course. More than ever, you're alert to your Team's timing, cues, and presence, and they're aware of how to answer in ways you'll immediately sense. Your mutual relationship has never been in a better place.

There are two ways that I encourage you to engage your Universal Team on a regular basis, and you don't have to subscribe to just one. Your first means of connecting is to set aside a regular block of time up to three days a week to use Believe, Ask, and Act as you've just learned—during meditation, prayer, writings, or in a quiet setting—and even return to the exercises in this book for guidance when you face a block related to the chapter's topic. The second option is to fold the three steps into the rhythm of your day as challenges arise. I tend to change my MO based on my time constraints and the issue's urgency, and you may want to do the same. Obviously, you can't clear a tornado block on the fly; it requires a strategy that's teased out during time with your Team. But if you have a quick question or face a thorny issue that demands a fast response, you can Ask in a more impromptu way. Suffice it to say that you'll feel instinctively drawn to the best method as you encounter situations that warrant it. And before you know it, you will not question the "hows" at all—it will become as natural as breathing.

You'll find, too, that because you have an efficiently working partnership with your Team and you're in tune with your gut, you will recognize and follow your Team's signs and opportunities without even asking for them! In each circumstance, you are fully navigating your journey with a honed intuition, which is precisely what God intended when He created you.

Perhaps the best way to illustrate this is to show what it's like to walk in the shoes of my longtime client Louisa. First thing in the morning, she says a quick prayer that affirms her beliefs and thanks God and her Team for their blessings—like her cat's health, her mom's sense of humor that yanks her out of a bad mood, and a sunny day ahead—then does a quick grounding and protection exercise to spiritually cover her to Ask all day long. On her way out the door, Louisa notices her bum knee is bothering her, so she Asks, *Who can help?* and feels a quick response to call her acupuncturist to see if she has an opening. She does this on her way to work, and once she's at her desk, her boss swings by for an update on a project. Louisa realizes she needs an extension and sets a meeting to discuss this. The meeting goes exceptionally well, and on her way out, Louisa notices a red robin on the windowsill—a sign she associates with her departed grandmother. Louisa smiles and thinks, Aww, *thanks*, certain that her Team had a hand in the meeting's outcome. An hour later, her acupuncturist calls back and says that she can see her at 2:00 p.m. This is a great "coincidence" since Louisa is in meetings all day, with the exception of 2:00 to 4:00 p.m. . . .

Like Louisa's, your Universal Team is with you at all times, guiding you to your best possible outcomes. Believe, Ask, and Act help you make choices based on faith, focus, and follow-through. Know, too, that using your instincts as a compass will never feel strained or laborious. Being limitless, in fact, is the very fluid intersection of your worldly intentions, thoughts, and actions with the universe's intentions, thoughts, and actions. It is a seamless blending of all that is. Thanks to your willingness to grow and your Team's ability to guide, you now have an improved capacity to love, be authentic, embrace the moment, move past doubt and fear, coexist with grief, respect your body, survive overwhelming circumstances, and comfortably step outside your comfort zone. This is a tremendous testament to your combined strength, and as a united front, you and your Team can achieve the impossible. What will you do next?

APPENDIX

During my own automatic writing sessions, I channeled the following reflections, meditations, and prayers. Each pertains to a chapter topic. You can recite them as you move through related blocks or turn to them for strength, encouragement, and reassurance whenever you need a little boost. I believe they came from different "specialists" on each subject because my handwriting changed every time!

Chapter 1: Coming Into My Own

I ask the light from up above
To show me the path of God's true love
And with each year of life I've lived
I outstretch my arms and have thanks to give
I learn to let go, no more doubt, no more fear
Express love and gratitude to those I hold dear
"Look within your heart" is what God says.
"Come with me and break the bread."
Close your eyes and listen to the words
Guided wisdom comes like songs to birds
Natural and free in all that you do
Choose the life that's meant for you.

Chapter 2: Your Role in God's Universe

Each and every one of us has a role to play
In our world, in the universe—now, today
Ask yourself, "How do I live?

What special gift do I have to give?"
Then set forth with all you have to show
Give unto others. Teach what you know.
Raise your vibration, set it up high
Then others around you, they too shall fly
It is with the quest to do all that you can
That you help in the universe's divine plan
And when you feel you have nothing to give
And the world's challenges seem all too big
Call on your soul and all that it knows
Ask for the knowledge to help this world grow
Follow a path that is true and full of love
And know you are part of the light from above.

Chapter 3: Meet Your Universal Team

Did you know that since your birth
An angel has been with you, here on earth?
A host of guides then by your side
Walking right next to you with every stride
With a gentle hand on your back
They try to fill spaces where you lack
Emotional strength or wisdom to give
Helping with the life you live
Decisions and heartache, sadness and more
Celebrations and joy, and love galore
This is your Team, filled with the best
From angels to Buddha, those put to rest
Jesus and Mary, animals too
You have a Team that's helping you
Sent on a mission from God's true light
Helping you make your path right
Call us when you need help and guidance
Strength, love, or to your path's compliance
It is with our power to guide in your life

Your job is to listen and to live your life right
Thank us when you know we are helping you
We beam with pride when you live your life true.

Chapter 4: Three Steps toward Enlightenment

Allow us this moment to explain to you
How it is that we help you do what you do
When the world outside just doesn't seem clear
We step in to help get rid of the fear
At first it might seem that all is lost
And life has dealt you a bitter frost
That's when it's time for you to lean
On all of us, your Universal Team
You're not alone, this you should know
We stay with you as you grow
So call upon us every day
Then listen to what it is that we say
A nudge, a push, a feeling of knowing
To take action in your life, to keep on growing
We can and will give you all of the signs
But it's you that has to start the climb
Trust in the world and universe alike
Know we can help to fight the good fight
Act on what we tell you then
That's when your life will start to mend
Know this thought and remember it to be true
That climb may not be easy to do
But when you reach the glorious top
Know in that moment you're not going to be stopped
A force, so strong, is who you are
Look at you! You've come so far
Bask in all that you've achieved
Be grateful for all that you believe
Trust in us, and all that it means
To have us beside you, your Universal Team.

Chapter 5: Start with Love

Dear God, I ask only this
That I find love in myself for a lifetime of bliss
It is with that moment that I accept myself
And understand that love is life's greatest help
All around I will extend an outstretched hand
Open my heart to my fellow man
And when it comes time for my heart's true mate
I will allow them in with little debate
For when I find love within myself
And understand life isn't power or wealth
I release myself to your loving will
And with your love, my heart will fill
I then can give myself to others
Lovers, friends, sisters, and brothers
Will all be part of what I have learned
That my love is more than free, it is gratefully earned.

Chapter 6: Practice Authenticity

With outstretched hands and a guided-up gaze
I ask this of you, help lift my haze
Allow me to be clear and true to myself
A being in light
Willing to serve and to help
Today I shed all my labels and marks
And look at myself in the light, no dark
With God's trusting hand and my guides' loving help
I stand here today, my true authentic self.

Chapter 7: Embrace the Now

It is with gratitude and peace within
That I accept this moment, and let go of where I've been
I worry not of what the future has in store

I smile at the past and close its loving door
Today I embrace the time I've been given
And appreciate the moment right now that I'm living
With angels by my side and a loving hand from above
I live in the now, full of glorious love.

Chapter 8: Move Past Doubt and Fear

Archangel Michael, I call for you here
Please help me with all that I doubt and I fear
I ask for God's light to shine from my heart
And lead me on the path I'm ready to start
It's with your guidance that I know only this
Doubt and fear will no longer stop my bliss
Today I move forward with you by my side
Guiding, protecting, shadowing my stride
I am ready to let go of all that I fear
With the help of my angels and loved ones near
I can conquer all of it is that I doubt
Because letting go of fear is what life is all about.

Chapter 9: Break Down the Great Wall of Grief

As I reached Heaven's golden door
With clouds beneath me as my floor
The sun now shined behind my back
And worldly woes, I now lack
An outstretched arm did come to greet
And all my angels I got to meet
One by one they showed me the way
On to a brighter and lovelier day
And when my mind thought, Wait, turn back,
I was told by my angel, these loving facts . . .
"Do not worry about all you've left behind
You'll be able to visit with sweet loving signs
You'll let them know that all is okay

With the signs that you give for what you can't say
At first they may question, Is this for real?
But after a while, they can't mistake what they feel
A presence, a nudge, a smell in the air
The feeling of knowing, yes, or beware
You will guide them my friend, just like before
You'll be able to watch them as their lives soar."

I thought about this, and I smiled real big
I knew the signs were real when I used to live
And as my angel stepped off to the side
There they all were, my loved ones who'd died.
Alive and well with a smile on each face
No hint of an illness or hurt, not a trace
And as they embraced my soul and loving heart
I learned, life goes on. We're never truly apart.

Chapter 10: Help Your Body Help You

Archangel Raphael, all I ask of you today
Is to help my body heal itself in each and every way
To have my soul join together with your loving, healing light
In fixing all that ails my body and having it work right
I ask for guidance in finding a healer on earth
Someone who has the knowledge to the answers I search
I pray to you for the strength I'll need to make it through each day
For love and light and all I need while on my healing way
With all my bodies fully aligned and ready to receive your grace
I ask to heal from my illness in a timely pace.
I express my thanks as I receive light in every fiber of my being
And know that I'll be positive and envision Spirit's healing.

Chapter 11: Survive Life's Twisters

My God, please show me the way
Of how to weather my storm today
I ask for the knowledge of what to do

With my full belief and trust in you
With your guidance I ask you this
Lead me toward my calming bliss
Allow my soul to see all things dear
To make my choices with my angels near
Knowing while I fight this fight
They are helping me make things right
And when I'm weak and all goes wrong
They'll be there cheering me on
I will rise up and look into the light
And thank you, God, for helping my life be bright
Healed and calm, your love so near
You give me the strength with nothing to fear.

Chapter 12: Leave Your Comfort Zone Behind

I have tried all I can, in all that I do
Today I accept that I must try something new
I ask my God for help, to let go of all I've known
And to lead me out of my comfort zone
Allow me to see all that I can achieve
Shoot for my dreams with no fear, truly believe
That all I dream will be waiting for me here
And reaching those goals is so very near
I promise today to my angels all around
Today I am ready to take big leaps and bounds
Changing my pattern and starting anew
Believing in me and eternally in you.

Chapter 13: Know You're Limitless

Having now seen the light, all my questions met
I learned that paths often vary and are never set
Although your soul in life may be predetermined
Don't think for one minute now, it's all the same sermon
Life will cast a spell on you if you allow the power

To be turned over to all that makes you cower
Hardships are your power tool instead of what holds you back
Fight the fight with all you've got and conquer what you lack
Tears may flow and hearts break, but this One knows for sure
Place your trust in God's hands, and He'll help you endure
You see, a promise to your God-earned gifts, it's not a lonely route
The universe wants us to be happy, that's what it's all about
Take this advice today, from Angels on high:
When you think you've had enough, we are here to help you try
At your side knowing your name and all that you need
Please remember one strong point—it takes us both to succeed
Hold my hand and I'll hold yours in a virtual state
Walk this path, me at your side, learning life's true fate
When you think you've had enough, all you can endure
Picture me, raising you up, giving you strength for more
And when that day comes to be, when a smile crosses your face
Live your life with gratitude, appreciate your place
This life is truly a gift to you, that's common ground for all
Remember when you need us, upon us you may call.

ACKNOWLEDGMENTS

"**L**et's write a book!" said my guides.

"How?" I asked.

"Say 'yes'—without fear, without doubt—and we will show you the path to take."

Well, let me tell you—they sure did deliver. But this book also could not have been possible without the support and love from the following people. I am abundantly grateful to you all.

To Kristina Grish, my coauthor and beautiful, treasured friend. Your professional guidance and personal enthusiasm throughout this book have been a gift to me in so many ways. Thank you for challenging me and, yes, my guides. It is because of you and your incredible talent that Spirit's voice can be heard alongside my own. Spirit sent you to me, and for that I am forever grateful. *BAA* is ours.

To my literary agent, Celeste Fine; Sarah Passick; and their team at Sterling Lord. You all have and continue to work with my best interest at heart. Thank you for opening your minds to the world of spirituality and for putting the time and effort into getting this book off the ground. Your support has been wonderful.

To my editor, Leah Miller; publicist, Yelena Nesbit; and the amazing team at Rodale. Your enthusiasm to delve into uncharted waters has been inspiring! Thank you for taking a chance on me and for believing in Spirit's words to help others connect and find balance in their lives. You have supported the message of this book from day one. I am so proud to be part of the Rodale team.

To Pat Longo, my spiritual teacher, healer, and close friend. It is because of you and your amazing gift that I am able to understand and process what Spirit shows me. You helped awaken me, and for that I am forever grateful. Thank you for all your love, guidance, and support. "The Dove spreads her wings, flies, and heals the world."

To my students, your inquiring minds keep Spirit and me on our toes. You are all beautiful light workers. You continue to help me learn how amazing Spirit can be.

To my clients—without you, this book wouldn't exist. Your stories continue to inspire my love for this work and drive to help others. I am humbled by and forever grateful for the opportunity to deliver messages from your loved ones and guides. Thank you for trusting me, sharing your time with Spirit, and believing in the divine process.

To my fantastic, supportive friends who, when I told them I was a psychic medium, supported me 100 percent. You have kept me grounded and laughing throughout this process! Thank you!

To my husband, Chris, and our beautiful family, Emily, Ryan, and Matthew, your love and support have made this process a joy. Thank you for your understanding and patience while I have worked on this book. I find true happiness within our family and home. I cherish each of you and love you all with everything my heart and soul have to give. And to my furry baby, Phoenix, who greets my clients and Spirit with his warm, calm demeanor and makes everyone feel right at home.

To my loving parents—all of them! Alice and Bob, Robert and Christine, you have guided and helped me mold myself and my life in so many ways. It's not easy having a psychic medium as a daughter! Thank you for opening your minds and showing me your love and pride. And to my brother, Anthony, and sister, Laura, who inspire me to do better in this life. You both continue to cheer me on through every hurdle and finish line. I love you both so very much! Thank you for all of your support.

And finally, to God, my guides, and my loved ones who live just beyond the veil. Thank you for allowing me to share this gift with others. You have provided me with the words that empower people to connect with Spirit so they can better navigate their lives. You have shown me the path to follow my own soul's true voice. For that and so much more, I feel incredibly blessed. I am humbled by the beauty and love you trust me to see and share in this world and beyond.

INDEX